TENNIS

CALMNESS

A Guide of Practical Strategies for

Self-Regulation in Competition

Alex Ivanov

Strategies for Juniors, Adults & High-Performance Competitors

TENNIS CALMNESS

A Guide of Practical Strategies for

Self-Regulation in Competition

Author: Alex Ivanov

© 2026

CONTENTS

FOREWORD

This book was not born in a library, nor from the sterile pages of an academic textbook. It was forged on the sunbaked courts of Australian junior tennis, in the middle of tiebreaks, through missed match points, and in the difficult silence of a long drive home after a tournament defeat that should not have happened.

But before any of that, before the tiebreaks and the long drives and the quiet frustration of a match that slipped away, there is something that must be said about why any of us are here at all. Tennis is fun. Genuinely, irresistibly, sometimes maddeningly fun. It has a way of getting under the skin that few sports can match - the satisfying crack of a clean winner, the geometry of a perfectly placed drop shot, the primal satisfaction of a first serve that nobody was returning. For many players and their families, it begins as a hobby and quietly becomes a way of life. Courts are booked before sunrise. Weekends are rearranged around draw sheets. Holidays are planned around tournaments. This is not a complaint; it is a confession that most tennis families will recognise immediately. The sport is addictive in the truest sense: the more you understand it, the more it reveals, and the more it reveals, the more you want. Yes, there are difficulties. Yes, there is drama. Yes, there will be moments when the emotional demands of competition feel disproportionate to what is, on paper, just a game. But that is precisely what makes tennis worth mastering. A sport that asks nothing of you gives nothing back. Tennis asks everything and in return, for those who embrace its demands rather than resist them, it offers something rare: a pursuit that is physically exhilarating, mentally sharpening, socially rich, and genuinely life-filling in ways that compound across decades. The health benefits alone (cardiovascular fitness, coordination, longevity) are well documented. The friendships forged on and around the court often last a lifetime. And the sheer joy of striking a tennis ball cleanly, of moving well and competing hard under open sky, never entirely goes away. Not at eight years old. Not at eighty.

My son began competing at a high level in Australian junior tennis from an early age. By his teenage years, he was a state-level competitor - technically gifted, tactically astute, and capable of dismantling opponents in practice that he would sometimes lose to in tournaments. His coaches admired his groundstrokes, technical execution, ability to read the court and his work ethic. His peers respected his athleticism and his ability to chase down every ball. His matches often drew crowds including school matches where other parents would leave their own child's court to watch my son and his insane ability to hunt down the hardest balls and get the highlight-reel worthy winners and angles.

And yet, when the pressure of some competition met the chaos of the court - the bad line calls, the external noise, the drama, the scoreboard - something would shift. Not in his body, but in his mind.

The game of tennis is deceptively cruel in this regard. It is a sport of extraordinary technical depth, yet one where the mental dimension often decides outcomes long before the final point is played. Unlike team sports, where a single player's psychological struggle can be absorbed or compensated by teammates, tennis places the individual in isolation. Every decision, every error, every challenge is yours alone. There is no one to pass the ball to. No team huddle. Just you, your opponent, a racquet, and the relentless judgment of the scoreboard.

For a junior competitor, this isolation is intensified by the uniquely stressful environment of self-adjudicated competition. In Australian junior tennis - as in junior competition around the world - players call their own lines. The system, while practical in its necessity, creates an environment unlike any other sport. Imagine thirty-two gymnasts competing for the same trophy, each one scoring their own performance. The potential for conflict, both genuine and deliberate, is ever-present. Do we really expect them to self-rate themselves anything other than a Perfect 10?

My son encountered all of it. He experienced opponents who 'hooked' - making deliberate bad line calls to steal crucial points. He played through the psychological noise of opponents' supporters speaking loudly within earshot, designed to break concentration. He competed against the added pressure of biased officials, parental expectation, the ego dynamics of junior competition, and the weight of his own ambition. He struggled with the frustration of shots that simply would not land where he envisioned them, with the injustice of opponents capitalising on pure luck, and with the physical toll of playing through fatigue, growing pains, and minor injuries.

None of these challenges are unique to him. They are the shared experience of competitive junior tennis players across every country, every level, and every age group. But acknowledging their universality does not make them easier to navigate in the moment.

Over the years that followed, we did what any determined family would do: we sought answers. We engaged sports psychologists. We sought out mentors - former players who had been through the fire of competition and come out the other side. We spoke with coaches including former Tennis Australia lead coaching staff and were fortunate enough to have conversations with players who competed on the ITF and ATP circuits, former Division 1 US college players and coaches, who shared their own experiences with extraordinary honesty. We read university-level sports psychology research and medical papers on the same topics to try and understand the impacts of performance under pressure. We tested strategies, discarded what did not work, and refined what did.

What emerged from that process is this book. 4+ years in the making. It is not a collection of borrowed theories. It is not a repackaged version of someone else's system. It is a practical, tested framework of strategies that real players - including my son - have used on real courts in real competitive situations to self-regulate, regain focus, and perform closer to their potential when it matters most.

The dream has not diminished. A Grand Slam is still the horizon. But we have come to understand that to reach the summit of professional tennis, the mountain must first be climbed from the inside. Technical mastery opens the door to elite competition. Mental mastery is what allows you to walk through it and stay.

This book is for every junior tennis player who has ever felt the match slipping away and not known how to stop it. It is for every parent watching from the fence, wanting to help but unsure how. It is for every coach who sees the talent but struggles to reach the mind. And it is for every adult competitor who knows the feeling of playing below their ability because the pressure of the moment proved greater than their preparation for it.

You may have already tried these strategies however may not be aware of the extent of the impact of such strategies on your body or nervous system or the extent of the connection with mindset control. This book is designed to give you a toolbox of strategies, try them out and take what works for you. Knowing you have multiple strategies available should circumstances change and you find yourself needing to adapt. We hope all readers can resonate and learn something from this book.

You are not alone in this. And with the right tools, you are more capable than you know.

~ We wrote this book because we wished we had such a guide for our son to help him navigate the intense and emotional moments of tennis. There was no consolidated playbook to help, so instead we tried it all, investing nearly ten thousand dollars into professional mental coaches, sports psychologists, tennis pros and ex-players, medical and psychological textbooks, and even into exercise physiologists in our attempt to understand the body-mind connection and help our son master his mindset. Some suggestions worked, a lot didn't, so we even undertook years of research to read psychology and medical published journals to try and understand this. After 4 years of navigating and trialling various strategies, we realised there is no 'one golden strategy', rather players need a toolbox of strategies they

understand and have practiced, so they have the option to assess and adapt to their differing emotions and circumstances.

A note on privacy: this book is published under a pen name. Where personal experiences are drawn upon throughout these pages including matches, moments, conversations, and the journey of our son as a competitor, names, locations, dates, and tournament details have been changed or omitted to protect the privacy of our son, his opponents, coaches, officials, and all others involved. This was not a decision we made lightly. It was made out of respect for everyone whose path crossed ours during those years, many of whom never asked to be part of a book. What has not been changed is the truth of what happened, what we learned, and what worked. The use of a pen name and the protection of identifying details do not diminish the authenticity of anything contained here. The strategies are real. The research is real. The journey that produced this book is real. Only the names have been changed, and that, we believe, is the right thing to do. ~

INTRODUCTION

The Pressure Cooker of Competitive Tennis

Tennis is not simply a sport. It is a sustained, repetitive test of self-control disguised as an athletic competition. Every player who has ever picked up a racquet and walked onto a tournament court knows this. The feeling is unmistakable - a tightening in the chest, a heightened awareness of every sound, a strange slowing of time around the important points, and a sense that the distance between executing a shot in practice and executing it under match pressure is far greater than the few metres between you and your opponent.

This book is specifically designed to address that gap - the distance between what you can do and what you actually do when the stakes are high. To close that gap, we must first understand why it exists.

The Sources of Frustration in Competitive Tennis

Junior tennis players - and adult competitors alike - face a category of challenges that is genuinely unlike those encountered in most other sports. These challenges fall into several distinct areas, each capable of disrupting performance in its own way, and often compounding one another during the same match.

Consistency and Its Absence

One of the most uniquely frustrating aspects of tennis is the relationship between effort and outcome. A player may hit a technically excellent backhand down the line that clips the tape and falls back in - an error rewarded with bad luck. In the very next point, an opponent's mishit floats over the net and lands within a centimetre of the baseline for a winner. Tennis punishes and rewards in ways that frequently bear no relationship to effort, intention, or skill.

For a junior player still developing emotional regulation, this randomness is deeply destabilising. Consistency - or rather, the inability to be consistent - becomes a source of profound internal frustration. You know how to hit the shot. You have done it a thousand times in practice. And yet on this day, on this court, in this moment, it is not happening. The forehand that is your biggest weapon becomes the stroke you most fear. The second serve that never gives you trouble suddenly feels as unreliable as a coin flip.

This kind of frustration is not a weakness. It is a normal human response to an inconsistency between expectation and reality. But it must be managed, because unmanaged frustration rapidly cascades into changed technique, reduced risk tolerance, and a narrowing of focus that serves only to increase error rates further.

Opponent Cheating and Self-Adjudication

Perhaps no aspect of junior tennis generates more emotional intensity than the self-adjudication system. In most junior tournaments, particularly at the domestic and regional levels, players are responsible for calling their own lines. This is a necessary practical arrangement - it would be impossible to provide qualified officials for every match at every tournament. But its consequences are significant.

The system creates an environment of inherent ambiguity. Line calls that are genuinely close become matters of subjective judgment. And where there is subjectivity, there is the potential for both honest error and deliberate manipulation. 'Hooking' - the practice of making a bad line call on an important point to gain a competitive advantage - is a reality of junior tennis competition. Any experienced junior player or coach will be able to name opponents they have encountered who use this strategy.

The psychological impact of being hooked is profound and multi-layered. First, there is the immediate injustice - losing a point you feel you won honestly. Second, there is the cognitive interference - the intrusion of anger and a sense of unfairness into the decision-making required for the next point. Third, there is the broader narrative that can develop - 'this opponent is going to keep doing this,' or 'I am not going to be able to beat them fairly' - which destabilises tactical thinking and shifts focus away from performance.

Learning to manage this aspect of competition is not about accepting injustice quietly. It is about recognising that your response to it is the only thing within your control, and that a compromised response costs you more than the bad call already did.

Environmental Pressures: Heat, Wind, Sun, and Glare

Tennis is one of the few major sports played exclusively in outdoor environments at the junior level, across a wide range of conditions. The Australian tennis calendar, in particular, exposes players to extreme heat. Competing in temperatures exceeding 35 degrees Celsius, often on concrete or synthetic hard courts that absorb and radiate additional heat, is physically and cognitively taxing in ways that are difficult to overstate.

Heat affects not only the body but the mind. Research in sport science consistently demonstrates that elevated core body temperature impairs decision-making, reduces reaction time, and increases perceived effort for any given workload. A player competing in the heat is not merely uncomfortable, they are operating with a meaningfully compromised cognitive system.

The physiological toll of heat extends further still. As the body works to cool itself through sweating, it loses significant volumes of water and essential electrolytes, particularly sodium, potassium, and magnesium. These electrolytes are not incidental to performance; they govern the electrical signals that control muscle contraction. When their levels fall too low, muscles become prone to involuntary cramping. This is a common and debilitating experience for tennis players in hot conditions, and it is worth understanding clearly: cramping is rarely a sign of weakness or poor fitness. It is a direct physiological consequence of fluid and electrolyte depletion, compounded by the sustained, repetitive muscular demands of tennis. A player who cramps late in a match in 38-degree heat has not failed, their body has reached a threshold that hours of intense effort in extreme conditions will reliably produce. Managing this risk requires proactive hydration well before play begins, consistent fluid intake during changeovers, and where appropriate, electrolyte replacement through sports drinks or supplementation.

Wind introduces a different challenge: unpredictability. A shot that would land comfortably in calm conditions may be carried long or dragged short by gusting wind. Toss control during serves becomes difficult. The sound of wind near the ears can mask auditory cues from the opponent's racquet strike. The net may appear to move. All of these factors introduce noise into the perceptual system, increasing the demands on the player's ability to adapt and focus.

Sun and glare present their own specific challenges, particularly during toss for serve or when tracking lobs. Playing into the sun on a critical point, when a high ball is simply lost in the glare, is a source of genuine frustration that sits entirely outside the player's control. Learning to manage the emotional response to these environmental variables, rather than resenting them, is a critical component of high-performance tennis.

Physical Factors: Fatigue, Growth, Injury, and Energy

Junior tennis players are, by definition, still growing. The physical demands of training and competing at a high level interact with the biological processes of adolescent development in complex and sometimes painful ways. Growing pains - the informal term for the musculoskeletal discomfort associated with rapid growth - are a genuine physical experience that can affect movement, confidence, and the ability to execute technically demanding shots.

Beyond growth-related discomfort, junior players regularly compete with varying levels of fatigue. Tournament schedules may require multiple matches in a single day. Travel, disrupted sleep, irregular meal timing, and dehydration can all impair physical and cognitive function. A player who arrives at a critical third-set tiebreak having already played for three hours is not the same player who walked onto the court at the start of the match. Managing performance across the physical arc of a match, and across the duration of a tournament week, requires both physical preparation and psychological skill.

Minor injuries - blisters, cramps, rolled ankles, muscle tightness - are a routine part of competitive sport. Learning to compete effectively through minor physical discomfort, without using it as a mental excuse for underperformance, is a skill that distinguishes developed competitors from developing ones.

Additionally, the physical factor of stress and burnout from a long or difficult day at school or work, or even life and home stresses, can present itself to players, impairing their ability to focus. Stress creates a mental and at times physical fatigue which can unduly impact cognitive functioning, decision-making, and emotional regulation, ultimately reducing a player's ability to stay present, execute skills effectively, and respond calmly under pressure.

Pressure from the Surrounding Environment

Tennis is rarely played in isolation. Parents, family, coaches, friends, opponents' supporters, and occasionally officials form a ring of observation around the court that can feel profoundly intimidating. The dynamics of this external environment are complex and frequently counterproductive.

Parental pressure - even when well-intentioned - can significantly distort a young player's relationship with competition. When a parent's emotional state becomes visibly tied to match outcomes, the player absorbs an additional layer of responsibility. They are no longer simply competing for themselves; they are managing the emotional state of a loved one from a distance of several metres. This is a burden that no junior athlete should carry, but many do.

Coach pressure takes a different form. The desire to demonstrate value, to justify the investment of training hours, and to not disappoint someone who has invested time and expertise in your development, can introduce a layer of performance anxiety that competes directly with the focus required for effective play.

Ego dynamics among junior players are pervasive. The culture of competitive junior tennis involves complex social hierarchies, rankings, and reputations. Losing to a lower-ranked opponent carries implications that extend beyond the match itself. Conversely, playing against a stronger opponent can trigger either underperformance through intimidation or overperformance through the absence of perceived pressure.

Opponents' supporters are an underappreciated source of psychological disruption. The practice of speaking loudly within a player's earshot - commenting on errors, discussing tactics, or simply creating social noise - is deliberately deployed in some junior competitive environments to interfere with concentration. An experienced competitor learns to recognise this tactic and build strategies to neutralise it.

The Execution Gap: Envisioning vs Delivering

Perhaps the most psychologically painful aspect of high-level tennis is the gap between what a player can imagine executing and what they actually produce in competition. Every player at the competitive level has a clear mental image of the shots they want to hit. They know where they want the serve to go. They know that the backhand should be struck through the ball with a full follow-through and aimed crosscourt. They know this because they do it in practice, regularly and reliably.

And yet, in competition, something interferes. The arm is not quite as free. The footwork is a half-step slower. The decision to change the shot is made a fraction of a second too late. The result is an execution that does not match the intention, and the frustration of knowing exactly what should have happened while being unable to make it happen is uniquely distressing.

Over time, many players begin to interpret this execution gap as evidence that they are mentally weak, unreliable under pressure, or somehow incapable of performing when it matters most. This interpretation is often more damaging than the missed shots themselves. The player stops trusting their game. They begin searching for technical fixes to problems that are psychological in origin, changing mechanics that were never truly broken. Confidence erodes not because ability disappears, but because the player no longer believes their ability will remain accessible under stress. The goal of mental training is therefore not to create a different player, but to restore reliable access to the player that already exists beneath the interference.

This gap is not permanent. It is not a reflection of permanent limitations. It is the direct result of the interference created by pressure, emotion, self-consciousness, and the disruption of automatic motor processes by conscious over-control. Understanding this is liberating, because it means the gap can be closed - not by practising the shots harder, but by developing the psychological skills to allow what has already been practised to emerge under pressure.

The scenarios and match situations presented throughout this book are drawn from real competitive experiences on the tennis court. They reflect genuine patterns of behaviour, emotional responses, and performance challenges observed across junior and adult play. However, to respect the privacy and confidentiality of all individuals involved, names, ages, locations, and identifying details have been deliberately altered. These examples are not intended to single out any player, but rather to provide realistic, relatable contexts through which the strategies in this book can be understood and applied in practice.

A Note on the Long Game

If you love this sport — or you are raising or coaching someone who does — do not let the scoreboard of early adolescence discourage you. The junior rankings are a snapshot, not a prophecy. The twelve-year-old who dominates their age group and earns a place at nationals, or the fourteen-year-old who is first in their state and travelling to junior ITF events, is not necessarily the player who will still be competing at the highest level at eighteen, twenty, or twenty-five. Development in tennis — physical, technical, tactical, and psychological — does not follow a straight line, and it does not follow a schedule. Some players peak early and plateau. Others develop slowly, quietly, and then arrive at their potential later than anyone expected.

The history of professional tennis is filled with players who lost consistently in their junior years, who were overlooked at fourteen and underestimated at sixteen, and who went on to compete at the highest levels of the game. What separated them was not that they won more junior matches. It was that they kept developing. They kept working on every dimension of their game — not just their groundstrokes and their fitness, but their mindset, their emotional resilience, and their ability to compete under pressure. Whether you are the player living this journey, the parent supporting it from the fence, or the coach guiding it from the sideline, the mental skills in this book are not a shortcut to success. They are part of the long, unglamorous, deeply rewarding process of becoming the most complete player you can be. Keep developing. Keep learning. Keep showing up. The journey is longer than any junior draw sheet can capture, and the story is far from written.

The Purpose of This Book

This book contains practical strategies, each independently researched and personally tested, for managing the mental and emotional demands of competitive tennis. The strategies are drawn from sports psychology, neuroscience, performance coaching, and the lived experience of competitive tennis across multiple levels of the game.

They are not theoretical abstractions. Each one can be applied during an actual match, in the space between points, without disrupting the flow of competition or drawing attention to itself. They are designed to be practised, embedded into routine, and deployed automatically when the pressure of competition demands it.

Whether you are a player struggling to perform in tournaments the way you do in practice, a parent trying to understand how to support your child's mental development in sport, or a coach looking for practical tools to add to your performance framework - this book is for you.

How to Use This Book

This book is written for three audiences: players, parents, and coaches. Whether you are the one standing on the court, watching from the fence, or designing the training programme, the strategies in these pages are for you. You do not need to read this book in any particular order, and you do not need to work through every chapter before the information becomes useful.

Think of the Table of Contents as your toolbox menu. Scan through it and notice which strategies you already use, which ones you have heard of but never tried, and which ones catch your attention. Even if a technique is already part of your game, there is value in reading its chapter. Research consistently shows that understanding *why* and *how* a self-regulation skill works — the physiology behind it, the psychology that explains it — makes that skill more deliberate, more meaningful, and more effective under pressure.

Some readers will choose to read from start to finish and refer back to specific chapters when a particular challenge arises in competition. Others will go straight to the chapter that addresses their most pressing problem right now, work on that one skill, and return for more when they are ready. Both approaches work. There is no right or wrong way to read this book, and no single chapter is a prerequisite for another.

What matters is not the order in which you read, but what you do with what you find. Take what resonates. Try it in training.

Build it into your routine. Come back when you need something different.

The court is a pressure cooker.

This book is your pressure valve.

PART ONE

BREATHING & BODY CONTROL

The breath is the fastest available tool for changing your internal state. Before any thought can form, before any strategy can be deployed, the breath is already at work - either activating your alertness or triggering your fight-or-flight response, or settling the nervous system into a calmer, more controlled state. The six strategies in this section teach you to take conscious control of a process that most players leave entirely to chance. Master your breath and movement, and you master the first layer of competitive pressure.

CHAPTER 1

Box Breathing (4-4-4-4)

> ♀ **PRACTICAL TIP:** Inhale for 4 counts, hold for 4, exhale for 4, hold for 4 - use this between points to immediately reduce your heart rate and regain composure.

What Is Box Breathing and Why Does It Work?

Box breathing - also known as four-square breathing or tactical breathing - is a structured respiratory technique that has been adopted by military special forces, elite athletes, surgeons, and emergency responders as a reliable method for regulating the autonomic nervous system under extreme pressure. Its name derives from the visual symmetry of its four equal phases, which can be imagined as the four sides of a square: inhale, hold, exhale, hold.

At the physiological level, this technique works by directly influencing the balance between the sympathetic nervous system - which drives the fight-or-flight stress response - and the parasympathetic nervous system, which governs rest, recovery, and calm. Under competitive pressure, the sympathetic system dominates. Heart rate rises. Muscles contract. Breathing becomes shallow and rapid. Cortisol and adrenaline flood the bloodstream. Decision-making narrows and becomes reactive.

Box breathing disrupts this cascade by forcing a conscious, rhythmic pattern onto the breath. The extended exhalation phase, in particular, stimulates the vagus nerve - a critical component of the parasympathetic system - triggering measurable reductions in heart rate and cortisol levels within as few as two to three breathing cycles. This is not metaphor or motivational language. It is measurable physiology, documented in peer-reviewed research in both clinical and sport performance settings.

The reason breathing techniques are so effective compared to many other forms of emotional regulation is that respiration occupies a rare position within human physiology: it is both automatic and consciously controllable. Most autonomic processes including heart rate, digestion, and hormonal release occur entirely outside voluntary control. Breathing, however, can function in both domains simultaneously. Under stress, breathing automatically accelerates and becomes shallow as part of the body's survival response. Yet unlike most autonomic reactions, the breath can also be deliberately slowed and structured through conscious intervention. This creates a unique access point into the autonomic nervous system itself. By voluntarily altering the rhythm of the breath, a player can indirectly influence processes that would otherwise remain inaccessible to conscious control, including heart rate, muscular tension, and emotional reactivity

The vagus nerve is the longest nerve in the autonomic nervous system, running from the brainstem down through the neck, chest, and abdomen. It acts as the primary communication highway between the brain and the body's major organs, including the heart, lungs, and gut, and is the central mechanism through which the parasympathetic system exerts its calming influence. When vagal tone is high, the body recovers quickly from stress, heart rate variability improves, and the nervous system returns to a regulated baseline faster after a spike. When vagal tone is low, as it tends to be in chronically stressed or overtrained athletes, the stress response becomes harder to switch off, and performance under pressure suffers accordingly.

The extended exhale phase of box breathing is the most direct available method for stimulating the vagus nerve without medical intervention. As the exhale lengthens, pressure changes in the chest trigger the baroreceptors (pressure-sensitive receptors in the blood vessels) which send a signal via the vagus nerve to the brainstem to slow the heart. This is called the baroreflex, and it is the physiological mechanism behind the immediate sense of settling that most people notice after a slow, controlled exhale. The hold phases at the top and bottom of the breath cycle compound this effect by extending the duration of vagal stimulation beyond what a normal breathing pattern would produce. For a tennis player, two full cycles of box breathing between points can meaningfully shift the nervous system away from the reactive, fight-or-flight state that competitive pressure produces, not through willpower or positive thinking, but through direct physiological engagement with the body's own regulation system.

For a tennis player, this means that within the twenty to twenty-five seconds available between points, it is genuinely possible to meaningfully alter your internal state. Not completely. Not permanently. But enough. Enough to take the edge off the spike. Enough to think more clearly.

Enough to execute the next point from a place of relative control rather than pure reactivity.

How to Perform Box Breathing on Court

The technique is straightforward in principle, though it requires practice to deploy effectively under match conditions. The sequence is as follows:

- Phase 1 - Inhale: Breathe in slowly through the nose for a count of four. The breath should fill the lower lungs first, with the belly expanding before the chest rises. This is diaphragmatic breathing, and it activates the calming mechanisms in the body more effectively than shallow chest breathing.

- Phase 2 - Hold: After the full inhale, hold the breath gently for a count of four. This phase builds a brief moment of internal stability, a pause before the release.

- Phase 3 - Exhale: Release the breath slowly through the mouth for a count of four. The exhale should be controlled, not forced. Imagine releasing tension through the breath, softening the muscles of the face, jaw, and shoulders as you breathe out.

- Phase 4 - Hold: At the bottom of the exhale, hold for a count of four before beginning the cycle again. This final hold reinforces the parasympathetic effect and establishes a rhythm.

On court, the full cycle can be completed once or twice between points depending on the available time. The technique is most effective when initiated immediately after the conclusion of a point - before the cognitive mind has had the opportunity to begin analysing or ruminating on what just occurred. The breath is your first move after every point, not your last resort.

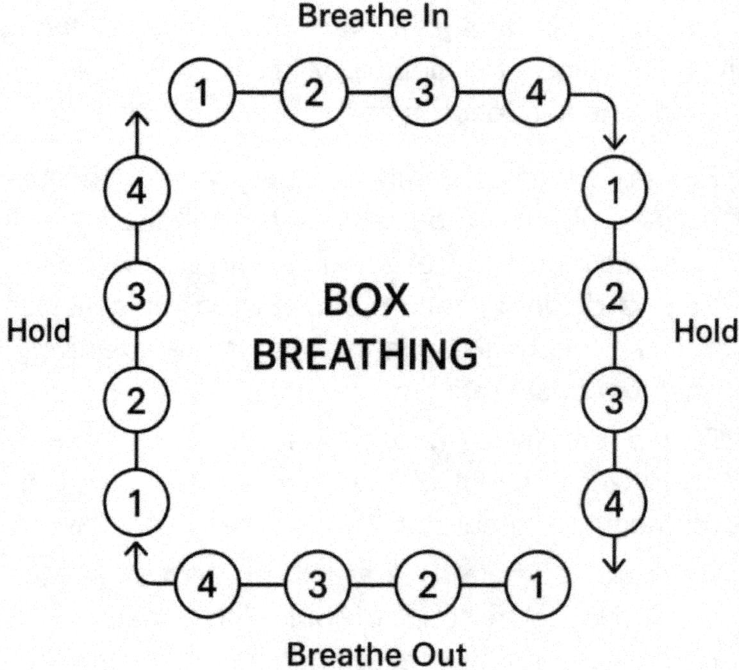

Training Box Breathing for Match Readiness

Box breathing is not a technique that can be successfully deployed under pressure for the first time during a critical match. Like any performance skill, it must be practised until it is sufficiently automatic to be accessible when the brain is operating under high cognitive load.

Begin by practising box breathing daily in a low-stress environment - before sleep, after waking, or during a quiet break. Establish the rhythm until it feels natural and does not require conscious counting. Once this foundation is solid, begin integrating it into training sessions, specifically at the moments when practice introduces pressure: after errors in feeding drills, between games in practice sets, or during the pause before executing a serve under a score constraint set by your coach.

The goal is to create an automatic association: pressure → breath. Not pressure → panic → breath as a remedy. The breath should be your immediate response to any emotionally charged moment, not a tool you reach for only when things have already escalated significantly.

Over time, this practice reshapes the relationship between competitive stress and internal state. Players who have trained box breathing consistently report a qualitative shift in how pressure feels - not the absence of stress, but a greater sense of control within it. The match still matters. The points still count. But the physiological spike becomes more manageable, and the window of clarity between the end of one point and the beginning of the next expands measurably.

Common Mistakes and How to Avoid Them

The most common error when first learning box breathing is forcing the breath rather than controlling it. The technique requires gentle discipline, not physical effort. If you find yourself straining to hold the breath or rushing the exhale, reduce the count to three for each phase until the rhythm becomes comfortable, then extend back to four.

A second common mistake is initiating the technique too late. If you wait until you are already in the middle of a panic or emotional spiral, box breathing becomes much harder to access effectively. Think of it as a preventive tool as much as a corrective one. Use it after every point - not just the difficult ones - so that your nervous system remains in a regulated range throughout the match rather than only after it has already spiked significantly.

Finally, avoid the mistake of rushing through the technique. The effectiveness of box breathing is proportional to the deliberateness with which it is performed. A hurried, mechanical version of the technique produces a fraction of the physiological benefit of a slow, intentional version. Quality of breath, not quantity of cycles, is what determines effectiveness.

★ REAL-LIFE EXAMPLE ★

The scoreboard read 5–6 in the final set. A junior competitor, deep into a state-level championship, was about to serve the most important game of his season. He had been here before - close to victory in the third set - and he had lost from here before. His body remembered this even though his mind tried to pretend otherwise.

The previous game had slipped away from him in a way that still burned. Two double faults in a row from 40-15 had brought him to deuce. He had tried to 'muscle' the ball into the service box and the effort had backfired spectacularly. His coach, watching from behind the fence, had seen the pattern: grip tightening, breathing shortening, posture collapsing. The technical breakdown was a symptom, not the cause. Unfortunately, the coach was unable to intervene or coach during this tournament, so there was no official way to flag the physical tightness to help him catch his mental spiral early.

The player walked to the baseline to serve and felt the familiar tightening in his chest. The crowd around the court - parents, friends, other players waiting for their own matches - seemed louder and more present than usual. He could hear his own heartbeat.

He bounced the ball five times before trying for his usually powerful kick serve. The ball kissed the net again. His opponent was smirking, obviously wishing for another double fault and the game. What better way to antagonise the server in such a precarious situation than to yell loudly "FAULT ONE" just to ensure everyone within a two-court radius could hear it. Thanks mate – now everyone knew, and the pressure grew.

He walked over to clear the ball from his court, tenseness rising and jaw clenching with frustration whilst darting hostile glances at his smug opponent. On his return to the baseline, he made a conscious effort to walk slower than usual to try the breathing technique he had been taught. That was the first deliberate choice. Rather than staring at the service box - at the target that felt impossibly small right now - he faced the back fence for a few seconds. He began the box breath.

In through the nose: one, two, three, four. The breath was slow and deliberate, filling his lungs from the bottom. He could feel his belly expand slightly before his chest rose.

Hold: one, two, three, four. There was a brief moment of stillness that felt strange given the circumstances. Out through the mouth: one, two, three, four. As the air left, he allowed his shoulders to drop. His grip on the racquet loosened fractionally. Hold: one, two, three, four.

He did not feel completely calm. He was not supposed to feel completely calm. But something had shifted. The urgency - that sharp, almost panicked quality of the previous game - had softened at its edges. He was still aware of what that moment meant, but the awareness felt less overwhelming. He was inside the moment now, rather than being consumed by it.

He turned back to face the court. He ignored his opponent swaying exaggeratedly like a pendulum whilst smirking like a sideshow alley clown. He focused on his breath, then bounced the ball, slowly, five times. He selected a target - wide to the backhand. He tossed the ball, struck it, and watched it land cleanly in the service box. The point unfolded, and while it was not without tension, he played it with a composure that had not existed a minute earlier.

The game went to advantage server. Then game - held. He walked to the net and tried not to show how much the single breath cycle had mattered. But he knew. It was not just the breath. It was the decision - in the middle of the highest-pressure situation of that match - to stop, to choose the breath, and to trust the process.

His coach, watching from the fence, made a quiet note. Not about the serve. About the turn, the pause, the deliberate breath. About the moment he chose regulation over reaction. That, more than the winner on the next point, was the development worth celebrating.

CHAPTER 2

Deep Inhale Through the Nose,
Slow Exhale Through the Mouth

> 💡 **PRACTICAL TIP:** A single deep nasal inhale followed by a long, controlled mouth exhale can interrupt a stress spiral within seconds - do this after any point that rattles you.

The Physiology Behind Nasal Breathing Under Pressure

The distinction between nasal and mouth breathing is not merely anatomical preference. It has meaningful physiological consequences, particularly under conditions of competitive stress. When we breathe through the nose, the air passes through structures that warm it, humidify it, and filter it before it reaches the lungs. More importantly for our purposes, nasal breathing activates the lower lobes of the lungs more effectively than mouth breathing, facilitating diaphragmatic engagement and, with it, greater parasympathetic activation.

Mouth breathing, by contrast, tends to be associated with shallow, chest-dominant breathing - the respiratory pattern of the stressed, reactive state. This creates a feedback loop: stress triggers mouth breathing, mouth breathing reinforces the stress response, and the cycle compounds. The deliberate shift to nasal inhalation breaks this loop at its physiological entry point.

Nasal breathing also increases the production of nitric oxide in the respiratory system, a molecule that helps dilate blood vessels and improve oxygen delivery to working muscles and the brain. During the recovery interval between points, this effect - even in miniature - supports both cognitive clarity and physical recovery. It is a small advantage, but in a sport defined by marginal gains, small advantages accumulate.

The Extended Exhale: Your Fastest Reset Tool

The exhale is where the real regulation happens. Research in respiratory physiology has consistently demonstrated that the length of the exhalation phase determines the degree of parasympathetic activation produced by any given breath cycle. An exhale that is longer than the inhale produces a greater calming effect than a balanced breath cycle. An exhale through the mouth, with slightly pursed lips - what respiratory therapists sometimes call 'pursed lip breathing' - further extends the duration of the exhale and increases the regulatory effect.

For a tennis player, the practical application is this: after any point that has generated a significant emotional response - whether from frustration, injustice, excitement, or anxiety - the single most effective thing you can do in the first three seconds is to take one slow nasal inhale and release it through a long, controlled mouth exhale. Not two cycles, not a full box breathing sequence (though that can follow). Just one breath, done with full intention.

The impact of this single breath on heart rate variability - a key indicator of autonomic nervous system balance - is measurable within the same breath cycle. The heart slows slightly. The shoulders may drop involuntarily. The jaw relaxes. The overall effect is a brief but meaningful reduction in physiological activation that creates a small window of clarity.

Integrating This Technique Into Your Between-Point Routine

This technique is most effective as the very first action taken after a point concludes - before turning away, before adjusting strings, before anything else. The moment the point ends, the breath begins. This immediacy is important because it pre-empts the onset of the cognitive loop - the mental replay of what just happened - before it has had time to establish itself.

The sequence should become automatic through consistent practice. Think of it as a reflex rather than a strategy. Your body will default to the stressed breathing pattern if the calming pattern is not strongly established. Training the reset breath involves deliberate practice in progressively more pressurised training contexts until the behaviour is reliably available under match conditions.

Coaches can support this development by building specific cuing into practice sessions. After every error in a drill, the player takes one slow nasal inhale and controlled exhale before responding. After every game in a practice set, same process. The objective is repetition - not of the technique itself in isolation, but of the technique as a response to competitive moments, so that the link between moment and breath becomes deeply conditioned.

Managing the Emotional Component

One important practical note: for this technique to be effective, it must be performed with genuine intention, not as a mechanical or performative action. Players who rush through a breath cycle without genuine engagement with the exhale will notice limited benefit. The quality of attention during the exhale is part of what makes it effective. Imagine, as you breathe out, releasing the previous point with the air. Not analysing it. Not replaying it. Releasing it.

What players often fail to recognise is that emotional spirals in tennis are usually sustained not by the original mistake itself, but by the continued allocation of attention toward it. The nervous system cannot fully settle while the mind remains cognitively attached to the previous point through replay, judgement, or self-criticism. Box breathing interrupts this attachment process. By deliberately narrowing attention onto the physical sensations of the breath with the expansion of the lungs, the slowing of the exhale, the feeling of air leaving the body, the brain is given an alternative object of focus. This attentional shift reduces the mental resources available for emotional rumination and allows the nervous system an opportunity to recalibrate before the next point begins.

This is not a metaphysical suggestion - it is a practical direction of attention. The breath gives you something specific to focus on during the exhale that is neither the previous error nor the upcoming point. It is a bridge of pure physiological attention, and it is available to you at any moment on any court in any match condition.

★ REAL-LIFE EXAMPLE ★

The wind had been gusting all afternoon, making the ball behave in ways that frustrated both players. The player had been working on patience all season, and today it was being tested relentlessly. The serve had been inconsistent - the toss drifting in the wind, the timing fractionally off on almost every point.

At 3-5, 30-40 on serve, he faulted his first serve, the wind picking up the ball and curving it outside the court by meters. Just my luck, he thinks. The crowd behind the fence - mostly parents, a few coaches - was quiet, but he could feel the weight of their attention. His coach had spoken to him about exactly this scenario. 'The second serve at break point is where you'll feel the most pressure,' he had said. 'And you need to know what to do when it happens.'

He knew what to do. He had practised it a hundred times. The question was whether he could access it when it mattered.

He turned and faced away from the opponent, directing his attention to the back fence on court. The first move was always the turn. He let the visual field of the court disappear from his peripheral vision. Then he breathed.

In through the nose. He felt the air moving slowly, filling from the bottom of his lungs upward. It was a physical sensation he had learned to pay attention to during practice - not the abstract idea of breathing, but the actual feeling of air moving through the body. Hold, briefly. Then the exhale - long, slow, through the mouth, lips slightly parted. He counted silently to seven before the air was gone.

He noticed two things: the tightness across his shoulders had softened, and the sound of the wind seemed less intrusive than it had a moment before. Both were small changes. Both were enough.

He returned to the baseline. He took a longer time than usual with the ball bounce - four bounces instead of two - matching each to the rhythm of the breath that had just settled his system. He selected a target, breathed out once more, gently, before beginning the service motion.

The second serve was struck with a shorter, more compact action than his usual motion - a deliberate adjustment for the wind conditions that his coach had been encouraging him to use on windy days. It landed cleanly, drawing a weak return that he put away with a confident forehand.

Deuce. He had survived. More importantly, he had made a clear, deliberate choice in the hardest moment of the match and executed it effectively.

The breath had become a reflex. Not a perfect one - there would be matches where he forgot, where the moment overwhelmed the habit. But today it was there when he needed it. That was progress that no scoreboard could fully reflect.

CHAPTER 3

Blow Out Tension: The Long Exhale Reset

> 💡 **PRACTICAL TIP:** A single long, deliberate exhale - audible or silent - physically releases muscular tension in the shoulders, arms and hands. Use it the moment a point ends.

Tension as a Performance Barrier

Muscular tension is the physical manifestation of psychological stress. When the nervous system perceives threat - whether physical or psychological - it triggers a systemic contraction of muscle fibres across the body. This is the biological preparation for action: tightened muscles are ready to fight or flee. In tennis, however, this same contraction works directly against the fluid, coordinated movement patterns required for effective play.

The paradox is that the harder a player tries under pressure - the more they want to succeed, and the more they perceive the stakes of the moment - the more likely they are to tighten, and the more that tightening will undermine the very execution they are trying to protect. Great effort and great tension are not the same thing, but they feel identical from the inside when you are in the middle of a pressure situation.

The long exhale provides a direct physiological interruption to this pattern. When the body is in a state of tension, the breath is typically held or shallowed. By consciously initiating a long, sustained exhale - pushing the air out of the body deliberately - the player activates the parasympathetic system, which counteracts muscular contraction and signals to the nervous system that the immediate threat has passed.

What the Long Exhale Does to the Body

The long exhale is distinct from normal breathing in its duration and intentionality. Where a typical resting exhale might last three or four seconds, a long exhale deployed as a tension release may last anywhere from six to ten seconds. This extended duration has several specific physiological effects.

First, it stimulates the vagus nerve more intensely than a normal exhale, producing a stronger parasympathetic response. Second, it physically reduces the activation of the muscles of the chest, neck, and shoulders - the primary sites of stress-related tension in most people. Third, it lowers heart rate variability in a way that is measurable even within a single breath cycle.

Fourth, and perhaps most practically relevant, it directs the player's attention away from the outcome of the previous point and toward a simple, controllable physical process. Attention cannot be in two places simultaneously. By fully engaging with the sensation of a long exhale, the player's attention is withdrawn from the mental replay of an error or the anticipatory anxiety about the next point.

When to Use the Long Exhale

This technique is applicable across a wide range of competitive situations but is particularly powerful in three specific contexts: immediately following a significant error, at the conclusion of an emotionally intense point (whether won or lost), and during the approach to the service line before a high stakes serve.

In the first context - following an error - the long exhale serves as an immediate interruption to the emotional escalation that typically follows a mistake. Rather than allowing frustration or self-criticism to take hold in the nervous system, the exhale redirects the body's response, creating a brief window in which composure can be re-established.

In the second context - after an intense point - the long exhale provides physical recovery as well as psychological reset. Extended rallies, in particular, generate genuine physiological fatigue, and the recovery interval between points is the only opportunity to address this before the next point begins.

In the third context - approaching the service line - the long exhale serves as the final element of the pre-serve routine, ensuring that the body enters the service motion in a relaxed, fluid state rather than a tense, contracted one.

The Role of Sound in the Exhale

Some players find that making the exhale slightly audible - a soft, controlled breath sound - enhances its effectiveness by adding a tactile and auditory dimension to the attention anchor. This does not need to be dramatic or performative. A quiet, almost inaudible exhale through slightly parted lips is sufficient. What matters is that the exhale is perceived by the player as a deliberate act of release, not merely a passive deflation of the lungs.

The sound also serves a secondary function: it signals to the body that the exhale is complete. When an exhale ends with a slight auditory conclusion, the nervous system registers a clear endpoint, which reinforces the sense of closure around the previous point.

A "friendly" doubles match between regular doubles partners had been tense from the first game. Although this match didn't count toward tournament points, it wouldn't impact any rankings, and there was no trophy or prize money on offer… both players were ranked closely, and their egos knew it. They were fighting for glory like Spartans, like it was the Wimbledon final in front of a crowd of 40,000 spectators.

He took the first set 7:6 and by the time the second set reached 4-4, the atmosphere on the small quiet suburban court had taken on a weight that felt disproportionate to the surroundings. Although only watched on by the birds in the trees aligning the nearby creek, they played like they were being televised on TV and trying to make highlight reels for Tennis TV.

He was playing the best tennis of his life and simultaneously making more errors than he had in months. The contradiction was familiar. High-quality hitting interspersed with inexplicable mistakes - exactly the pattern that had cost him matches all year. His forehand was producing some genuine winners, but every two or three games, he would tighten at a crucial moment and sail the ball long or into the net.

At 4-4, 15-30 on his opponent's serve, he found himself at the net after a well-constructed approach shot. The pass came - wide to his forehand volley. It was the shot he had practised a thousand times. He reached, made contact, and dumped it into the net from a metre inside the service line. 30-30.

He felt the tightening immediately. Not just frustration - actual physical contraction, spreading from the base of his neck across his shoulders and down through his forearms. His grip on the racquet had tightened involuntarily during the miss, and he became aware of it now as a kind of locked-up heaviness in his right hand.

He turned away from the net. He began to walk back to the baseline, and as he walked, he exhaled. Not a dramatic sigh - just a long, steady release of air through his mouth, pushing the tension outward with the breath. He counted the duration silently and reached eight before the exhale was complete. His shoulders, he noticed, were slightly lower than they had been before the exhale. His grip on the racquet had softened.

He reached the baseline and stood for a moment. He took a normal breath in, then exhaled again - long and deliberate. The tightness across his shoulders was still there, but it had softened at the centre of it. The rigid quality had become something more like ordinary tiredness, which was manageable.

The point that followed was not won. His opponent hit a strong serve that he could only block back weakly, and the ball was put away. But this was soon followed by deuce on the next point, and then by a game-deciding error from the opponent on the next. The game went his way.

The breath had not fixed the match. It had not corrected the missed volley or taken away the frustration. But it had interrupted the escalation that typically followed that kind of error, and in doing so it had preserved the possibility of the game-turning point that came next. Sometimes in tennis, preservation is everything.

CHAPTER 4

Drop Shoulders Consciously

> 💡 **PRACTICAL TIP:** After every point, consciously let your shoulders drop. This single action resets upper-body tension and signals calm to your entire nervous system.

Why the Shoulders Are the Tension Barometer

Of all the sites where stress accumulates in the body, the shoulders are among the most revealing. The trapezius muscles - which run from the base of the skull, across the shoulders, and down to the mid-back - are among the first muscles to contract in response to psychological stress. This is an ancient biological response: when threatened, the body raises and tightens the shoulders as part of the protective reflex that evolved to shield the neck.

In a tennis context, this manifests as a creeping elevation of the shoulders during the course of a competitive match. A player who begins the match with relaxed, low shoulder position gradually develops a slightly hunched, elevated posture as the match progresses and pressure increases. This change is so gradual that it frequently goes unnoticed - by the player, by coaches, and by parents - until it has already impacted performance significantly.

The practical consequences for tennis technique are substantial. Elevated shoulders restrict the range of motion of the serving arm, reducing racquet acceleration and consistency. They interfere with the trunk rotation required for effective groundstrokes. They tighten the forearm, reducing wrist freedom and, with it, the ability to generate spin. They also affect breathing: tight, raised shoulders encourage shallow chest breathing, which compounds the physiological stress response.

The Mechanics of the Conscious Shoulder Drop

The deliberate shoulder drop is exactly what its name describes: a conscious, intentional release of the muscles that hold the shoulders in an elevated position. It is not a shrug - a shrug involves deliberate muscle contraction before release. The shoulder drop begins with awareness: noticing that the shoulders have drifted upward and then choosing to release them downward.

The action itself takes less than two seconds. The player simply allows gravity to do its work, releasing the contraction in the upper trapezius and deltoid muscles. Many players find it helpful to accompany the shoulder drop with a slow exhale, so that the physical release of tension synchronises with the respiratory release. This combined action - exhale plus shoulder drop - produces a stronger regulatory effect than either technique alone.

The sensation is often described as surprising in its completeness. Players who have been carrying elevated shoulders for a prolonged period frequently report that, upon consciously dropping them, they feel as though they have released a weight they did not realise they were carrying. This is the accumulated tension of competition, made visible through a single deliberate action.

Building the Shoulder Check into Your Routine

Consistency is the key to extracting maximum benefit from this technique. The goal is to make the shoulder check - and the associated drop if needed - an automatic component of your between-point routine rather than an occasional corrective measure deployed only when tension becomes severe.

A practical way to build this habit is to pair it with another routine behaviour that already occurs reliably. Many players find that the walk to the back fence provides the ideal opportunity for a shoulder check. As they walk, they become aware of shoulder position, release any elevation, and allow the shoulders to settle before they stop and begin the next phase of their routine. The movement of walking provides a natural context for the release.

Players at a more advanced stage of development may find that a simple self-cue - a word, a touch of the shoulder with the non-racquet hand, or a specific visual reminder - is sufficient to trigger the check automatically. The development of this automaticity is the goal: a shoulder drop that happens without conscious deliberation, as part of the trained response to the end of each point.

His dad and coach saw it from twenty metres away. Not the error - the error was visible to everyone - but what came before it. The shoulders creeping upward during the rally. The swing getting shorter. The footwork becoming more cautious. All of it visible in the body before the ball ever went into the net.

The player was playing the best competitor in their age group. He was competing brilliantly, but it was a difficult match against his opponent who was first seed. To make it worse, this tournament was a 1 set decider with Monrad draw knockout.

In the first set he held the lead at 5-2, something he has never done before against this particular opponent, and something he surprised himself with as this was not expected against such a higher ranked and arguably more capable player. He was on a roll, thinking he's "got this!!" and thinking about how it will propel him through to the next round and through to a good chance of winning that huge trophy.

However, something changed at 5-2 even though he felt more confident. He lost the next 3 games in a row due to his own unforced errors. He couldn't work out why all of the balls were now going long, wide and into the net. He almost had the set but now it was 5-5 and he was getting desperate. He absolutely had to win the next game. He wanted to beat this opponent and wanted to progress to the next round.

His dad, watching from the players' area, had seen this pattern before: physical composure gradually eroding through the pressure of a match he desperately wanted to win.

The first tiebreak point allowed for a long rally but his ball went into the net on a backhand on a short ball - the kind of setup that in practice he would punish without hesitation. Under this pressure, his shoulders were so far up toward his ears that his swing had no room to move freely. The ball hit the tape and fell on his side.

On the changeover that followed, his dad kept it simple. Although he couldn't communicate with him, he mimicked the body movement he was missing, in the hopes he would notice him and copy. Inhale and then deep exhale whilst dropping his shoulders as far down as possible. He sat there breathing like he was having a medical episode, with the straightest posture and his head held high and shoulders lowered.

The player became aware of his dad's actions and understood the cue, releasing his shoulders. They were, genuinely, somewhere near his earlobes. He almost laughed at himself. He dropped them - a full, conscious release - and felt the immediate loosening of everything above the waist. His neck seemed longer. His breathing deepened involuntarily. His arms felt lighter.

He walked back onto court and implemented it immediately. After the next point of the tiebreak - a long rally he lost the point narrowly - he walked to the fence, checked his shoulders, dropped them, and exhaled. They had already begun to rise again.

The pattern over the next few points was remarkable. His shot quality improved, not because he changed anything about his stroke mechanics but because his body was suddenly free to move the way it already knew how to move. The backhand that had gone into the net appeared again - not on a short ball this time, but on a run-around from the backhand corner - and this time it flew crosscourt for a clean winner.

Although he lost the match in the tiebreak, he was able to maintain enough focus to not spiral out of control. He kept pace with his opponent and lost overall 6-5. Although not a win, the score was exceptional given the disparity in experience and the spread of the rankings between them.

CHAPTER 5

Shake Out the Arms

> 💡 **PRACTICAL TIP:** A quick, deliberate shake of the arms and hands between points releases neuromuscular tension instantly - think of it as resetting your body's grip on the previous point.

Understanding Neuromuscular Tension Accumulation

During the course of a competitive tennis match, the muscles of the forearm, wrist, and hand are in a state of near-continuous activation. Even during the recovery intervals between points, residual tension persists in the musculature of the hitting arm. This is partly due to the metabolic demands of repeated muscle contraction, and partly due to the elevated sympathetic nervous system activity that characterises competitive play - a state in which baseline muscle tone is higher than it would be at rest.

Over the course of a long match, this accumulated tension is one of the primary contributors to the technical degradation that many players experience in later stages. The forehand that was fluid and powerful in the first set becomes tight and erratic in the third. The serve that was consistent in the warm-up becomes unreliable at 5-4 in the deciding set. Players and coaches frequently attribute this to fatigue, but in many cases the primary driver is not muscular exhaustion but neuromuscular tension - a state in which the muscle remains partially contracted even when it is not actively working.

The Mechanics of the Arm Shake

The arm shake is a simple, brief, bilateral movement in which the player allows the arms - from the shoulder down to the fingertips - to hang loosely and move in a rapid, oscillating motion for two to three seconds. The movement should be completely passive: the arms are not actively moved but rather allowed to swing freely from a loose shoulder joint. The wrists and fingers remain soft throughout.

This action produces an immediate reduction in residual muscle tension through a mechanism related to the muscle spindle reflex. The passive oscillation of the arm at a speed that prevents sustained muscle contraction effectively resets the baseline activation level of the forearm and hand musculature, restoring the loose, fluid limb state associated with effective tennis stroke production.

Many players discover this technique intuitively - it feels good, and it produces a noticeable improvement in arm freedom almost immediately. The deliberate, trained version of the technique simply makes what might otherwise be an inconsistent habit into a reliable, automatic component of the between-point routine.

Combining With the Shoulder Drop and Breath

The arm shake is most effective when combined with the shoulder drop described in the previous chapter. The sequence - exhale, drop shoulders, shake arms - addresses the entire upper kinetic chain in a coherent, progressive way. The exhale relaxes the chest and begins to soften the shoulders; the shoulder drop releases the upper trapezius; and the arm shake completes the release all the way down to the fingertips.

This full sequence takes approximately five to seven seconds and can be performed during the walk to the back fence following any point or from end changeovers. When practised consistently, it becomes one of the most reliable tools in the player's recovery arsenal - not because it is dramatic or complex, but because it directly addresses the sites of tension accumulation with a targeted, efficient physical action.

Four hours into a school team competition, the player had played two matches and was about to begin a third. At the age of thirteen he was the team's most consistent player.

His arm had been feeling tight since the first match. Not injured - just heavy, slow, slightly unresponsive in a way that is difficult to describe precisely but immediately recognisable to any player who has experienced it. His forehand was catching the frame more often than usual. His serve felt as though it was being struck with a wooden arm rather than a fluid, relaxed one.

His mother had watched him during his second match and noticed that he was holding the racquet unusually tightly. His swing seemed to unnaturally rotate his body with it. She mentioned it to the team coach, who nodded. This was a known pattern: fatigue not in the muscles but in the nervous system, manifesting as tension held in the shoulders, hand and forearm.

During the pre-match brief for his third match, the coach called him over under the pretence of checking if his over grip needed replacing. He told him quietly to shake his arms out before every game. Not once - before every game, and after every point where the arm felt tight.

He implemented it immediately and felt slightly ridiculous doing so for the first two points. By the third point, the arm had begun to feel different. Not completely loose - the fatigue was still there - but the locked-up quality had reduced. He was generating more racquet head speed with less apparent effort.

He won all of his matches in straight sets that day. After the last point, he walked to the net with his arm hanging loosely at his side, fingers uncurled, and his opponent looked slightly surprised at the casualness of the movement. He was not being casual. He was being deliberate.

The shake-out had become, in the course of one match, part of his recovery routine. He knew he would need to maintain it, practise it, and build it into his regular between-point habits. But the discovery itself was worth more than the match result: the realisation that his body, under pressure, was holding tension it did not need to hold, and that a two-second physical action could meaningfully release it.

CHAPTER 6

Relax Grip Pressure on the Racquet

> 💡 **PRACTICAL TIP:** Consciously soften your grip between points - a lighter grip produces better feel, more spin, and greater racquet head speed when it matters most.

The Grip as the Interface of Pressure

The grip is where the player's nervous system meets the racquet. It is the most direct physical expression of internal state during a tennis match: a player's grip pressure fluctuates in real time with their emotional and physiological state. Under low pressure, grip pressure tends to be moderate and variable - tightening naturally at the moment of contact, then releasing during recovery. Under high pressure, however, grip pressure tends to become uniformly elevated, remaining tight through the entire point and the interval between points.

This uniform elevation of grip pressure is one of the most common and most damaging consequences of competitive stress in tennis. It restricts wrist freedom, reduces racquet head speed, impairs the feel required for touch shots, and ultimately results in exactly the kinds of errors the player is trying hardest to avoid. The tighter you hold the racquet when you are anxious, the less effectively the racquet behaves - a cruel feedback loop that many players experience but few fully understand.

Under pressure, this tightening response is not accidental - it is physiological. The stress response naturally increases muscular tension throughout the body, particularly in the hands, forearms, shoulders, and jaw. The nervous system interprets competitive pressure as a form of threat, preparing the body for protection and force production. Understanding this helps players recognise grip tension not as weakness, but as a normal stress reaction that can be consciously regulated.

Optimal Grip Pressure and Its Benefits

The concept of optimal grip pressure is well-established in tennis coaching. The classic analogy - attributed to various sources - is to hold the racquet as though it were a small bird: firm enough that it cannot fly away, loose enough that it is not harmed. This metaphor, while simple, captures something technically accurate: the racquet performs best when it is held with enough tension to maintain control but not so much that it cannot move freely through the air.

A lighter grip allows the wrist to snap through the hitting zone more effectively, generating greater racquet head speed and, with it, more spin and pace. It allows the strings to dwell on the ball fractionally longer, improving the feel of the shot and enabling better directional control. It also enables faster adjustments to unexpected ball trajectories - the wrist remains mobile and responsive rather than locked in position.

Grip pressure is also useful because it provides immediate physical feedback about a player's emotional state. Emotions can be difficult to identify in the middle of competition, but excessive tension in the hand is often easy to notice. A consciously softer grip between points can therefore act as a simple reset mechanism, interrupting rising tension before it spreads more broadly through the body and mind.

Beyond the mechanical benefits, a consciously lighter grip produces a psychological effect: it signals to the nervous system that control is being exercised from a place of skill rather than force. The instinct under pressure is to grip tighter - to try harder, to hold on. Releasing the grip - deliberately, consciously - is an act of trust in your own ability and preparation.

How to Monitor and Reset Grip Pressure

The challenge with grip pressure is that its elevation under stress is largely unconscious. Most players do not think 'I will tighten my grip now.' The tightening happens automatically, driven by the sympathetic nervous system, and remains invisible until it has already compromised performance.

The solution is to build a routine grip pressure check into the between-point interval. After turning away from the court, the player briefly becomes aware of the racquet in their hand: How tight is the grip right now? Do the fingers feel relaxed or contracted? Is there tension in the forearm? This awareness check takes only a second, but it provides the information needed to make a deliberate adjustment.

If the grip is found to be elevated, the correction is simple: open the hand briefly - releasing the racquet slightly or simply uncurling the fingers - before re-establishing the grip at a deliberately lighter pressure. Some players find it useful to transfer the racquet to the non-dominant hand between points specifically to allow the hitting hand to fully release its grip. This is a valuable habit that also supports the broader arm-shake release described in the previous chapter.

He was playing doubles in the regional school final championships, in the deciding rubber of the team competition. He was serving at 5-6 in the final set. He had never competed at this level of significance before, especially representing his school. The result of this match would determine which school advanced to the state championships. There was pressure everywhere around the court as teammates lined against the fence and parents and coaches watched from the stands unsuccessfully trying to hide their nerves. Every point seemed to carry the weight of the entire afternoon.

His partner noticed the signs building gradually through the second set. His grip on the racquet had been tightening progressively, almost like he was trying to choke the life out of it. His first serves, normally reliable, had begun to veer wide by narrow margins. His topspin backhand had flattened out, travelling lower and faster through the court with less shape and margin than usual. The harder he tried to control the ball, the less naturally the racquet seemed to move. These were the signs of someone fighting with their racquet rather than using it.

He bounced the ball once, then caught it again instead of serving. His partner shuffled closer and said quietly: 'Loosen your hand. Just your hand.'

It was not a random comment. It was the exact instruction they had practiced together after their coach had explained grip pressure the previous month. At training, they had spoken about how pressure often travelled first into the hand and forearm before it spread to the rest of the body. Under stress, he naturally squeezed tighter, his muscles tightened, and his strokes lost their natural flow.

He looked at his partner, then at his own right hand, which was gripping the throat of the racquet with a whitened intensity that he had not even realised was there.

He transferred the racquet into his left hand. He opened his right hand as wide as possible, stretching all five fingers outward until the tension across the palm became obvious. He held it there briefly - one second, two seconds - before reaching for the racquet again.

When he re-gripped the handle, he did so consciously, at what felt like seventy percent of the usual tension. Loose enough that it initially felt uncomfortable. Light enough to feel strange.

Something shifted immediately. Not completely, but enough.

The serve that followed was struck with a pace and shape he had not produced for several games. Not because his technique had suddenly improved, but because the wrist and forearm had been freed to do what they already knew how to do. The ball kicked high to the returner's backhand side, drawing a defensive return that floated short into the middle of the court.

He stepped forward and put away the forehand volley cleanly.

Deuce.

Then advantage.

Then game, set, match.

The team erupted along the fence line behind the court. His partner grabbed him around the shoulders while teammates spilled through the gate in celebration. For several moments, the noise and movement blurred together into something almost difficult to process.

Later, once things had settled, their coach pulled the pair aside and asked quietly what his partner had said before the serve.

They explained the adjustment.

'That is worth a hundred forehand drills,' the coach said. 'You already know how to hit the ball. The job in a pressure situation is to stop preventing yourself from doing it.'

He wrote that phrase in his Tennis Match Journal notebook later that evening. He would re-read it many times over the following year, in many different circumstances - not all of them on a tennis court - and continue finding new meaning in it.

PART TWO

BETWEEN-POINT ROUTINES

The twenty seconds between points is not dead time. It is the most important time in the match. How you use it determines who you are when the next point begins. The eight strategies in this section give you a structured, practical toolkit for turning that interval into a performance advantage.

CHAPTER 7

Turn Away from the Court Immediately After a Point

> 💡 **PRACTICAL TIP:** The moment a point ends, turn your back on the court. This simple physical action interrupts rumination-the tendency to replay mistakes, overanalyse outcomes, and stay mentally stuck on the last point-and creates a clear psychological boundary, allowing you to reset, refocus, and prepare for what comes next.

Among all the strategies available to a competitive tennis player, the act of immediately turning away from the court following the conclusion of a point is one of the most deceptively simple and profoundly effective. It requires no equipment, no significant time, and no particular athletic ability. What it requires is a decision - a consistent, trained decision to disengage from the visual field of the court before the brain has the opportunity to begin replaying what just happened.

The reason this matters lies in how the brain processes performance errors and emotionally charged events. When a player remains facing the court after a lost point, every element of the playing environment - the net, the opponent, the ball rolling away - continues to serve as a sensory trigger for the memory of what just occurred. The brain's pattern-matching system uses these visual cues to reconstruct and replay the error, often generating an increasingly emotionally amplified version of events with each repetition of the loop.

By turning away, the player removes these triggers. The visual field changes completely. The opponent is no longer visible. The site of the error disappears from the player's sensory environment. This does not erase the memory - nothing can do that - but it removes the ongoing stimulation that would otherwise maintain and amplify the cognitive and emotional response.

The Immediacy Principle

The critical word in the strategy is 'immediately.' A delayed turn - taken thirty seconds after the point, once the cognitive loop has already begun to consolidate - has a fraction of the interrupting power of an immediate turn taken within the first two seconds of the point's conclusion. This is because cognitive loops around performance events follow a predictable escalation curve: they begin small and grow rapidly. Interrupting the loop at its origin is far more efficient than attempting to halt it once it has gained momentum.

The immediate turn is effective partly because it replaces reaction with procedure. Under pressure, players often remain facing the court after a missed shot, visually and mentally locked into the error. The physical act of turning away interrupts this fixation pattern. It creates a brief separation between the completed point and the next one, signalling to the brain that the event is over and no longer requires active processing. In this sense, the turn is not avoidance, it is controlled disengagement.

Developing the immediate turn requires repetition. It must become an automatic response to the conclusion of every point - not just the difficult ones, not just after errors, but universally. This universality is important for two reasons. First, it means the behaviour is consistent and therefore becomes more automatic over time. Second, it means the brain does not have to make a judgment call about whether a given point 'deserves' a turn. Every point ends with a turn. The decision is made in advance and therefore does not consume cognitive resources in the moment.

★ REAL-LIFE EXAMPLE ★

During the ages of 10 and 11, he had a very specific problem when playing tournaments. Both he and his coach knew exactly what it was. After a bad point - particularly an unforced error - he would stand motionless for several seconds, staring at the exact spot where the mistake had happened. Sometimes his eyes stayed fixed on the net tape where the ball had clipped. Other times they drifted toward the section of court where the ball had landed long or wide. By the time he finally walked back into position, almost the entire between-point interval had already been consumed by replaying the error in his mind.

The same pattern appeared on close line calls. If an opponent called the ball out - especially on shots he believed had clipped the line - he became trapped in the moment. He would stare toward the mark and ask the same questions every time.

'Are you sure?'

'Are you *really* sure?'

'By how much?'

'Show me the mark.'

Even after the discussion ended, his attention often remained fixed on the previous point rather than the next one. The frustration was not only about losing the rally. It was the feeling of injustice that lingered afterward, especially when he believed the call had been dishonest.

His coach had tracked the pattern carefully over several tournaments and noticed something striking. His win-loss record in the first game immediately following a break of serve or major mistake was almost completely inverted compared to the rest of the match. When he was playing freely, he competed exceptionally well. But after a significant error, the following game was often his weakest stretch of tennis.

The issue was not technical. It was attentional.

Recently, his coach had introduced a concept called the immediate turn and made him practise it repeatedly during training sessions. The rule was simple: the moment the point ends - the instant the second bounce occurs, the ball lands out, the opponent hits a winner, or an out call is heard - he turns his back on the court immediately.

Not after watching where the ball landed.

Not after analysing the mistake.

Not after questioning a line call.

Immediately.

The first training session with the rule felt surprisingly uncomfortable. He found it genuinely difficult to turn away before his brain had completed its assessment of the point. The urge to examine the error was powerful. He wanted to understand exactly what had gone wrong, how far the ball had missed by, whether the opponent's call had been fair.

His coach pointed out gently that this exact urge was what had been costing him the next game after major mistakes for nearly two years.

The turn itself did not erase frustration. He still felt the missed forehands. He still disagreed with close calls. But the turn interrupted the spiral before it could fully establish itself.

Within three training sessions, the movement had started becoming relatively automatic. Within three weeks, opponents, parents, and other coaches watching his matches began noticing something different about his demeanour between points. His reactions appeared steadier. He seemed almost identical after a missed forehand and after a clean winner.

Internally, this was not entirely true. The emotions were still there. But the immediate turn prevented those emotions from dominating his behaviour and, more importantly, the quality of the next point.

His coach tracked the numbers again over the following tournament season and noticed the pattern had completely shifted. The game immediately after a break of serve was no longer his weakest game. In several matches, it became his strongest.

Not because he had changed his strokes.

Because he had changed what he did with the fifteen seconds between points.

CHAPTER 8

Walk to the Back Fence

> 💡 **PRACTICAL TIP:** Always walk toward the back fence after a point - the physical displacement creates mental distance from what just happened and gives your body time to reset.

Walking to the back fence is a behavioural strategy that transforms the natural recovery interval between points into an active regulation exercise. By deliberately moving away from the central playing area and toward the perimeter of the court, the player achieves several things simultaneously: physical displacement from the previous point's location, temporal spacing between the end of one point and the preparation for the next, and an embodied sense of transition.

The physical act of walking is itself a form of self-regulation. Movement engages the motor system of the brain, which in turn draws cognitive resources away from the rumination loop and toward the processing of movement itself. This is not merely theoretical: research in clinical psychology consistently demonstrates that physical movement is one of the most reliable methods for interrupting cycles of repetitive negative thought. In a tennis context, the brief walk to the fence may be one of the simplest and most accessible applications of this principle.

For many players, the back fence gradually becomes psychologically associated with reset and regulation through repetition. Over time, consistently walking to the fence after points conditions the brain to recognise that location as a cue for decompression, recovery, and emotional recalibration. This is one of the reasons routines become so powerful in competitive sport: the nervous system begins responding not only to the action itself, but to the repeated meaning attached to the action. Eventually, the walk to the fence ceases to be merely movement across the court and becomes a conditioned signal to settle, reset, and prepare again.

Pace, Posture, and Intention

The quality of the walk matters as much as the destination. A player who rushes to the back fence - driven by urgency or agitation - does not derive the same benefit as one who walks deliberately, with a measured, controlled pace. The walk should feel purposeful but unhurried. The shoulders should be relaxed (ideally dropped consciously, as described in Chapter 4), and the head should be upright rather than lowered.

This combination of measured pace and composed posture has a regulatory effect on the nervous system through the pathway of embodied cognition: the brain reads the body's movement quality as information about the overall state of the situation. A composed walk tells the nervous system that the situation is manageable. An agitated rush tells it the opposite. The player is not merely moving from one location to another; they are performing composure, and in doing so, cultivating it.

The junior team championships had an unusual dynamic. Matches were played on adjacent courts with full visibility between teams. Players watched their teammates compete only metres away, calling encouragement across fences and reacting audibly to momentum swings. Every hold of serve, every missed volley, every disputed line call seemed to attract an audience. The environment added a layer of social pressure that made each match feel larger than its individual significance would normally warrant.

The player had been drawn against the number one player from the opposing team - a physically imposing opponent nearly eighteen months older and nationally ranked for his age group. He already looked years ahead developmentally. There was a dark shadow across his jawline, thick forearms, broad shoulders, and the kind of effortless power that made even routine groundstrokes sound heavier off the strings. From the outside, he appeared completely unaffected by pressure.

Early in the match, though, the younger player had competed brilliantly. He took the ball early, redirected pace confidently, and raced through the opening four games of the first set. For a short period, the match had unfolded exactly as he wanted.

Then, gradually, the momentum shifted.

Over the next three games, he lost his grip on the match in a way that felt strangely outside his control. The errors themselves were not catastrophic, but the space between points began disappearing. He stopped resetting. He stopped separating one rally from the next.

His teammates watching from the adjacent court noticed it before he did.

Normally, he walked all the way back to the fence between points, using the movement to slow himself down and mentally reset. Now he was doing the minimum possible. A few steps behind the baseline. A quick turn. Then immediately preparing for the next serve or return. There was no transition period anymore. Each point bled directly into the next without any psychological boundary between them.

The pace of the match began controlling him.

It was not a technical problem but a collapse in behavioural pacing. Under pressure, the player had unconsciously shortened the transition between points, removing the very space that normally allowed his nervous system to regulate itself. Without that recovery interval, emotional carryover accumulated rapidly. Frustration from one rally leaked directly into the next point, and the match began unfolding faster than his ability to mentally process it. The instruction to walk to the fence was therefore not symbolic or motivational - it was an attempt to deliberately rebuild the psychological boundary between points.

At the changeover, the team coach walked over quietly and crouched beside the chair. He offered only one instruction.

'After every point, walk to the back fence. Touch it. Then walk back.'

There was no long explanation. No tactical discussion. Not enough time for that. But the coach said it with enough certainty that the player accepted it immediately.

The second set carried a noticeably different rhythm.

Not because he suddenly played flawless tennis. The opponent was still bigger, stronger, and capable of taking control of rallies whenever short balls appeared. But now every point followed the same clear structure: play the point, turn away, walk to the fence, touch the fence, walk back, prepare again.

The fence became a physical checkpoint. Something fixed and reliable inside an environment that had started feeling rushed and unstable.

The effectiveness of the routine came partly from its physical simplicity. Touching the fence provided a concrete action that anchored attention externally rather than internally. Instead of remaining absorbed in analysis, self-criticism, or emotional reaction, the player's focus briefly shifted toward movement, space, and sensory contact. In performance psychology, these small physical anchors are often highly effective because they interrupt spiralling cognitive loops without requiring complex conscious thought. The body performs the routine first, and the mind gradually follows.

With each walk, the tempo of the match slowed slightly. The emotional residue of the previous point had less opportunity to carry forward. By the middle of the second set, his body language had steadied noticeably. He was no longer reacting impulsively to errors or hurrying between points.

He still lost the match.

The older opponent was simply too strong on that particular day, and no adjustment to routine was going to completely bridge that gap. But afterward, the coach noted something far more important than the scoreline.

The progressive deterioration from the first set never reappeared.

He competed through the second set with a consistency of effort and composure that had been absent once the momentum shifted earlier in the match. He stayed emotionally present on each point, even when losing games.

And when he walked off court, he knew exactly what needed further development. Not a groundstroke. Not a serve. Not his tactical awareness.

Merely a simple habit - the walk to the fence.

CHAPTER 9

Tap the Back Fence

> 💡 **PRACTICAL TIP:** When you reach the back fence, tap it once with your hand. This tactile anchor marks the boundary of the previous point and physically grounds you in the present moment.

The tap of the back fence is a simple, tactile punctuation mark on the between-point reset process. It takes less than a second. It requires nothing more than the willingness to make deliberate physical contact with a stationary surface. And yet, when practised consistently, it performs a function that is both neurologically and psychologically significant.

Tactile contact with a stable, fixed surface activates sensory receptors in the skin and underlying tissue, generating sensory information that the brain processes as evidence of physical stability. This is a form of grounding - in the most literal physical sense. The fence does not move. It is solid and fixed. By touching it, the player's nervous system receives a moment of unambiguous physical reality that can interrupt the abstract cognitive loops of match pressure.

The tap also serves as a deliberate ritual marker. Human beings use rituals - structured sequences of behaviour with clear beginning and end points - to manage transitions, whether in sporting, cultural, religious, or social contexts. The tap of the fence marks the end of the walk, and with it, the end of the active disengagement phase of the between-point routine. What follows the tap - the preparation to return to the baseline - is a different phase, with different cognitive content.

The Psychology of Deliberate Ritual

Research in sport psychology consistently demonstrates that pre-performance and between-performance rituals reduce performance anxiety and improve execution consistency. The mechanisms are multiple: rituals reduce decision-making load (because the sequence of behaviours is pre-determined), they provide a sense of personal control in an uncertain environment, and they create a cognitive context of preparation that primes the player for the demands of the next point.

Part of the effectiveness of ritual also lies in predictability. Competitive tennis is psychologically demanding partly because so much of the environment is uncertain: outcomes fluctuate, momentum shifts rapidly, and players cannot fully control what happens next. Rituals introduce small islands of certainty into that uncertainty. The player knows exactly what they will do after each point, regardless of the score, the previous error, or the emotional state they are experiencing. This consistency creates stability within instability, which helps reduce cognitive chaos under pressure.

The fence tap, within this framework, is not superstition. It is purposeful behaviour. The player does not tap the fence because they believe the fence possesses any power over the outcome of the match. They tap it because the act of tapping it is a trained signal - to themselves, to their nervous system, and to their routine - that the reset phase is progressing as designed, and that the next phase will begin from a regulated baseline.

★ REAL-LIFE EXAMPLE ★

The fence tap had developed almost accidentally.

During a regional coloured-ball competition when he was ten years old, he had lost an important point after missing an easy forehand. Frustrated, he walked to the back fence and placed both hands and his racquet gently against the chain-link as though pushing himself away from the moment. It was not something he had planned or been taught. It simply happened.

A coach watching nearby noticed it afterward and asked what he had been doing at the fence.

'I don't know,' he answered honestly.

'Then do it every time,' the coach said. 'Not just when you're frustrated. Every single time you go to the fence.'

Over the following years, the fence tap gradually became one of the most reliable anchors in his between-point routine. From the outside, it appeared insignificant - just a brief touch against the fence before returning to position. But internally, it carried a very specific feeling that he came to trust.

He could never have fully explained to an outsider why it worked. What he could describe, though, was the sensation in the moment: a brief encounter with something solid and predictable that interrupted whatever noise was building in his head and brought his attention back to the physical reality of the court.

By the age of fifteen, the habit had become automatic.

During a state-qualifying tournament, he faced an opponent who had been making consistently questionable line calls throughout the second set. The calls existed in the difficult grey area that makes such situations so frustrating - not obviously incorrect enough to formally challenge, but repeatedly marginal and somehow always favourable to the caller on important points.

Late in the set, a crucial first serve down the T was called out. He knew immediately the ball had clipped the line.

Even from the far side of the court, the frustration in his body language was obvious. His jaw tightened sharply. His grip on the racquet changed almost instantly, fingers clamping harder around the handle. He took several quick steps toward the mark before stopping himself.

Then he turned and walked to the fence.

He placed one hand flat against the cold chain-link metal. He could feel the texture pressing against his palm. He leaned slightly into it, feeling the resistance of something stable and unmoving beneath his hand.

He held it there for two seconds. Something shifted.

Not the injustice itself. The frustration did not disappear. He still believed the call had been wrong. But the emotion became contained rather than consuming. By placing his attention briefly onto something external and physical, the frustration lost some of its ability to occupy his entire mental space.

When he walked back to the baseline, his breathing had steadied slightly. His shoulders had lowered. More importantly, his decision-making remained intact.

Instead of forcing aggressive low-margin shots out of anger, he adjusted tactically. He aimed with larger margins over the net, extended rallies, and trusted that the opponent's consistency would eventually break down if points became physical and patient enough.

He won the next three points and held serve. Soon after, he won the set.

Later, reflecting on the match, his coach noted that the outcome had depended less on technical execution than on a small physical action performed at precisely the right moment. The fence tap had interrupted what could easily have become a downward emotional spiral.

By recognising the rising frustration early and grounding himself physically before it escalated further, he prevented a legitimate grievance from turning into a match-defining collapse.

CHAPTER 10

The Towel Ritual: Wipe, Breathe, Release

> 💡 **PRACTICAL TIP:** Use your towel between points as a multi-tool reset: wipe your hands or face, cover your face briefly for a silent release of frustration, and breathe deeply before returning to the baseline.

More Than a Piece of Cloth

The towel hanging on the back fence or the net post is one of the most under-utilised performance tools in a tennis player's arsenal. Most players treat it as a practical hygiene item - something to wipe sweat from hands or face in warm conditions. And it serves this practical purpose effectively. But with deliberate intention, the towel can also serve as a portable, always-available reset station: a location to visit, a physical process to engage in, and a sequence of actions that can meaningfully alter a player's internal state between points.

Physical objects often become psychologically powerful in sport because they provide something concrete for attention to anchor to under pressure. During emotionally heightened moments, the mind tends to become internally crowded with thoughts, predictions, frustrations, and self-monitoring. Interacting with a simple external object - such as a towel - redirects attention outward into a controllable physical process. This shift away from internal mental noise and toward structured physical action helps interrupt emotional escalation and creates a temporary sense of order within the unpredictability of competition.

The strategic use of the towel involves several distinct components, each of which serves a different regulatory function. Together, they create what can be thought of as a micro-restoration sequence - a brief but comprehensive address of the physical and psychological residue of the previous point.

Wiping Hands or Face: The Physical Reset

The simple act of wiping hands or face with the towel has both practical and psychological value. Practically, it removes the sweat and moisture that can compromise grip quality and ball toss precision. Psychologically, it provides a deliberate, repetitive physical action that directs attention away from the previous point and toward a simple, controllable present-moment task.

The intentionality of the wipe matters. A rushed, perfunctory wipe-down provides minimal psychological benefit. A slow, deliberate wiping of each hand - attending to the sensation of the towel against the skin, the dryness of the grip it leaves, the brief pause it provides - creates a more meaningful moment of attention. Some players find that wiping the face also serves as a brief moment of privacy: with the towel against the face, the visual field of the court disappears, and there is a moment of genuine sensory withdrawal.

The Towel Over the Face: Privacy for Emotional Release

One of the challenges of tennis is that it is played in full public view. Every expression of frustration, every visible sign of anxiety, every moment of apparent vulnerability is visible to the opponent, coaches, parents, and spectators. This visibility creates an additional layer of self-consciousness that can compound the pressure of the moment.

Placing the towel briefly over the face - as though wiping perspiration from the forehead and eyes - creates a momentary privacy screen. In this brief private moment, the player can release frustration in a way that would otherwise be visible and potentially disadvantageous. A silent expression - a clenched jaw, a brief exhale, a momentary facial expression that authentically reflects the internal emotional state - can be performed without it being observed or interpreted by opponents or officials.

This technique is not deceptive or performative. It is a practical accommodation of the reality that genuine emotional regulation sometimes requires a moment of private expression. The towel provides that moment. Some players also find it useful to combine the face-covering moment with a pinching of the nose - a technique used in breathwork to create pressure that, upon release, triggers a deeper nasal breath and a subsequent calming parasympathetic response.

Breathing While Using the Towel

The most important element of the towel ritual is the breath that accompanies or follows it. Whether the player is wiping hands, wiping face, or using the towel as a brief privacy screen, the breath should be deliberate throughout. The reset breath described in Chapter 2 - deep nasal inhale, long mouth exhale - is ideally suited to the towel moment. The towel provides the context; the breath provides the regulation.

Players who develop this combination - towel plus breath - as a consistent between-point habit report that the towel becomes, over time, a conditioned stimulus for the calming response. The act of picking up the towel begins to trigger the parasympathetic response automatically, even before the breath is consciously initiated, because the brain has formed a strong associative link between the towel and the state of regulation that has reliably followed its use.

The sun was brutal. It was an Australian summer tournament late in the morning, and the hard-court temperature had already been measured at 37 degrees Celsius by the tournament director, who was monitoring conditions for potential heat policy enforcement. The heat radiating upward from the court felt heavier than the air itself. The humidity only intensified it. Sweat gathered constantly on racquet grips, strings, hats, wrists, and eyebrows. Both players relied heavily on their towels between points.

But there was a clear difference in how the towels were being used.

The opponent treated his towel purely as equipment management. He would walk quickly to the fence, swipe it once across his forearm or neck, drop it back over the fence, and immediately return to position. The entire process lasted only a few seconds.

The player had been taught to use the towel differently.

After every point - regardless of whether he won or lost it - he walked deliberately to the back fence and followed the same sequence each time. First, he dried each hand individually, paying attention to the feeling of dryness returning to his palms and fingers. Then he brought the towel gently to his forehead and eyes, blocking the court from view for several seconds.

In that brief moment of visual withdrawal, he exhaled slowly. The towel had become more than a way to manage sweat. It was part of the reset.

In the sixth game of the third set, his opponent produced three consecutive winners from deep behind the baseline. Each shot was struck cleanly and aggressively - heavy crosscourt forehands followed by a flat backhand winner down the line. They were not tactical mistakes or poor decisions from the player. The shots were simply too good.

Still, the emotional impact of losing three rapid points in succession - particularly to winners of that quality - carried obvious danger. Momentum in tennis can feel psychological long before it becomes tactical. Lesser competitors often allowed sequences like this to accelerate internally, carrying frustration and helplessness directly into the next point.

At 0-40 on serve, the player walked calmly to the fence once again. His pace did not change.

He removed the towel from the fence and pressed it gently across his face. For several seconds, the court disappeared completely. The opponent, the heat, the parents watching from outside the fence - all of it vanished behind the fabric. He exhaled slowly into the towel.

His jaw clenched once, briefly and privately, before relaxing again. There may even have been a few muffled words hidden inside the towel itself - frustration released quietly where nobody else could hear it. A short swear word. Then:

'Come on.'

'You got this.'

When he lowered the towel, his breathing had steadied. He returned to the baseline and began again.

Point by point, he rebuilt the game. After every rally, regardless of outcome, he returned to the towel. Wipe hands. Cover face. Exhale. Reset.

He won the next four points and held serve from 0-40.

From outside the court, his coach could not hear what had been said beneath the towel or fully know what had happened during those hidden moments. But he recognised the pattern immediately.

Towel.

Pause.

Reset.

Perform.

CHAPTER 11

Adjust Strings Slowly

> 💡 **PRACTICAL TIP:** Take five seconds to straighten your strings between points. The slow, deliberate act directs your attention onto something controllable and away from the previous point.

Racquet string adjustment is one of the most commonly observed between-point behaviours among professional and high-level amateur tennis players. What appears to an untrained observer as a habitual or almost absent-minded fidgeting behaviour is, for many players, a deliberate attentional reset strategy. When performed with genuine intention - slowly, with full awareness of the tactile feedback from the strings - it functions as a powerful micro-mindfulness exercise in the middle of a competitive match. In a sport defined by rapid emotional fluctuations and constant evaluation, the ability to anchor attention in something simple, repeatable, and controllable becomes a competitive advantage. String adjustment can be that structured, purposeful and timed event to create the psychological break between points.

Part of the power of repetitive tactile behaviours lies in their predictability. Under pressure, the mind is often pulled toward uncertainty - future outcomes, previous mistakes, changing momentum, or fear of consequences. Small repetitive actions such as adjusting the strings provide the nervous system with something stable and familiar to return to. The consistency of the sensation and movement creates a brief pocket of certainty within an otherwise unstable environment, helping the player regain a sense of grounding and continuity between points.

The effectiveness of string adjustment as a reset strategy derives from several mechanisms. First, it provides a specific, task-oriented focus for the hands and eyes during the between-point interval - a concrete alternative to the default cognitive activity of replaying the previous point. Without such an anchor the mind tends to drift toward rumination, self-criticism or tactical over-analysis. Second, it engages the tactile sensory system, grounding the player in immediate physical experience. The feel of the strings - their tension, alignment, and resistance - brings awareness back into the present moment, interrupting unproductive thought loops. Third, it introduces a period of fine motor control, which activates neural pathways associated with deliberate, controlled action rather than reactive behaviour. This shift from reactive to intentional movement subtly reinforces composure and control.

Importantly, the value of string adjustment is not in the complexity of the behaviour, but in its simplicity. High-pressure situations tend to overload conscious thought processes, making complex mental instructions difficult to execute reliably. A simple physical task that can be repeated identically under stress is far easier for the brain to access consistently. This simplicity allows the behaviour to remain effective even when emotional intensity is high and cognitive resources are reduced.

Beyond its psychological value, string adjustment also serves a practical and performance-related function. Correcting the alignment of the strings helps maintain a consistent and predictable string bed response at contact. Misaligned strings can alter how the ball interacts with the racquet face, subtly affecting spin generation, control, and feel. While the performance impact of minor misalignment may be small in isolation, over the course of a match - particularly in high-level play where margins are extremely fine - consistency of contact becomes critical. By routinely straightening the strings, players reinforce a sense of equipment reliability, which in turn supports confidence in stroke execution. The action becomes both a physical calibration and a psychological reassurance: the racquet is prepared, and so is the player.

Regular inspection of the strings during adjustment also provides an important preventative benefit. High intensity play places significant stress on strings, leading to fraying, notching, and eventual breakage. A player who habitually engages with their strings between points is more likely to notice early signs of wear - loose fibres, thinning areas, or sections that have shifted excessively. Recognising these indicators allows for mental preparation if a break is imminent, reducing the shock and disruption that can occur if a string snaps unexpectedly during a critical moment. In some cases, it may also inform tactical decisions, encouraging slightly more conservative shot selection until a racquet change can be made. This awareness contributes to a broader sense of control over both equipment and environment.

Speed as a Diagnostic Tool

An interesting secondary benefit of the string-adjustment strategy is that the pace at which a player adjusts their strings serves as a reliable real-time indicator of their internal state. A player who is racing through string adjustment, fingers moving quickly and imprecisely, is almost certainly in a heightened state of arousal - often accompanied by increased heart rate, muscle tension, and narrowed attentional focus. Conversely, a player who is moving slowly and methodically is demonstrating a degree of internal regulation, allowing their physiology and attention to settle between points.

Coaches who learn to read this indicator can use it as a subtle but powerful coaching cue, even without verbal interaction. Observing the tempo and quality of a player's string adjustment can provide insight into their emotional state, helping guide between-set conversations or post-match feedback. Players themselves, once aware of this pattern, can use their own string adjustment pace as a self-monitoring tool. If the strings are being adjusted hastily, that is not just a habit - it is information. It signals a shift in internal state and provides an immediate opportunity to intervene. By consciously slowing the movement - feeling each string, aligning them with intention - the player can actively down-regulate their arousal level and re-establish control.

Over time, this simple behaviour can evolve into a reliable personal ritual - a consistent bridge between points that reinforces routine, presence, and composure. In high-pressure environments where external variables cannot be controlled, small, repeatable internal processes like string adjustment become anchors. They provide structure amidst chaos, helping the player return, point after point, to a state where clear thinking, effective decision-making, and controlled execution are once again possible.

★ REAL-LIFE EXAMPLE ★

He had been training under his current coach for nearly three years when the string-adjustment ritual was introduced, and his first reaction was openly sceptical.

'It's not going to change anything,' he said. 'It's just moving strings around.'

His coach did not argue. Instead, he asked him to commit to using it for one full practice session before deciding whether it was useful or not. Reluctantly, the player agreed.

The instruction itself was simple: after every point, before doing anything else, he was to straighten at least three strings on his racquet. Slowly. Deliberately. Full attention on the feel of the strings beneath his fingertips.

No rushing. No absent-minded tapping. Actual attention.

At first, it felt pointless. He adjusted the strings mechanically, mostly because he had been told to. But as the session continued, something subtle began happening. The act itself demanded enough concentration that it interrupted the normal replay loop that usually followed mistakes.

Instead of mentally reviewing missed forehands or analysing whether a tactical decision had been correct, his attention shifted toward something immediate and physical: the tension of the strings, the alignment, the small tactile movements beneath his fingers.

By the end of the session, he still did not make any dramatic claims about the technique. However his coach noticed something immediately. He had been noticeably steadier between points than usual.

When the coach pointed this out afterward, the player shrugged casually. 'I didn't really think about the last point,' he admitted. 'I was thinking about the strings.'

That was precisely the point.

Two months later, during the regional championships, he encountered a match that became progressively more emotionally difficult as it unfolded.

His opponent was a highly consistent baseline player who had recognised midway through the first set that the player's composure was more vulnerable than it initially appeared. Gradually, the opponent began manipulating the tempo of the match within the limits of the rules.

Between points, he moved slowly. The ball bounces before serving became exaggerated and prolonged. Hats were adjusted repeatedly. Shoelaces seemed to require constant re-tying. Towels took longer to use. Every transition stretched slightly beyond what felt natural.

During rallies and after points, the opponent's celebrations also grew louder and more theatrical. Fist pumps became more exaggerated. Calls of 'Come on!' echoed deliberately across nearby courts. It was the familiar catalogue of subtle competitive mind games players often use in an attempt to get inside an opponent's head.

Against many players, the tactic worked effectively. The prolonged waiting disrupted rhythm and slowly built frustration, but against him, something unexpected happened. The opponent's delays simply gave him more time with his strings.

After every point, while his opponent extended the pauses intentionally, the player lowered his attention calmly toward the racquet in his hands. He straightened the strings slowly and methodically, almost like someone focused on fine craftsmanship. He worked carefully to align the vertical and horizontal lines as neatly as possible.

He was no longer standing there waiting impatiently for the opponent. He was occupied.

The longer the pauses became, the more opportunities he had to reset.

By the middle of the second set, the opponent's attempts to disrupt rhythm had begun losing their emotional effect entirely. The player remained composed between points, emotionally flat in the best possible way, moving through the same deliberate sequence each time.

He won the match in straight sets.

Afterward, his coach made a quiet note to discuss the match during the debrief. Not because the routine itself was tactically brilliant - it was not. The action was extremely simple. But it demonstrated something important – a strong between-point routine is not merely a reaction to pressure. It becomes a buffer against it.

CHAPTER 12

Bounce the Ball Deliberately

(Serve Routine)

> 💡 **PRACTICAL TIP:** Establish a fixed number of ball bounces before every serve and keep the pace consistent - this rhythmic anchor stabilises your internal state and commits your body to the upcoming action.

The serve is unique in tennis in one crucial respect: it is the only shot over which the player exercises complete initial control. The pace, the placement, the timing of initiation - all of these are entirely in the server's hands. This theoretical control, however, frequently becomes a source of pressure rather than a resource, because the server must initiate action from a standing start, in a moment of silence, with full awareness of the stakes. Without a structured process, this pause can amplify tension and overthinking. With a well-rehearsed routine, however, it becomes a controlled entry point into performance - a moment the player owns rather than fears.

The ball bounce ritual - the sequence of bounces that precedes the serve - is the primary mechanism for managing this transition from stillness to action. When performed deliberately and consistently, it creates a rhythmic bridge between the between-point reset and the execution of the serve, allowing the player to enter the service motion from a prepared, regulated state rather than a static, anxious one. Just as importantly, the consistency of the ball bounce routine provides the player with something stable and repeatable under pressure - a part of the performance that remains unchanged regardless of score, opponent, or environment. In a sport full of variables, this small element of control becomes psychologically grounding.

Rhythm as Regulator

The rhythm of the ball bounce is not arbitrary. It should match the player's current desired internal tempo. Under normal conditions, the bounce tempo reflects a calm, ready state. Under pressure conditions, there is a natural tendency for the bounce tempo to accelerate - to rush through the routine in response to the perceived urgency of the moment. When the player notices this acceleration, it is a signal to deliberately slow the bounces.

This deliberate slowing is a form of tempo regulation. By controlling the pace of the bounces, the player establishes the internal tempo they wish to carry into the service motion. A slow, measured bounce sequence tells the body: we are unhurried. We have time. This execution will be controlled rather than rushed. The body, trained through repetition, translates this message into a serve that reflects the same qualities. Over time, this link between bounce tempo and serve execution becomes conditioned, allowing the player to use rhythm as a reliable lever for performance under pressure.

Consistency as the Foundation of the Routine

The specific number of bounces a player uses is less important than the consistency of that number. Rafael Nadal's pre-serve routine has been studied extensively by sport psychologists as a model of ritual-driven self-regulation. While players need not emulate his exact sequence, his routine demonstrates a broader principle: high-level performers build comprehensive, repeatable rituals that extend beyond the ball bounce itself. Nadal's routine includes not only a consistent number of bounces, but also a precise sequence of behaviours - adjusting his shirt, tucking his hair behind his ears, wiping his face - all performed in the same order before every serve. These actions are not superstitions; they are structured cues that guide the mind and body into a familiar performance state.

Players should establish their own version of this routine in practice - whether it involves two, three, or four bounces, combined with simple physical cues - and maintain it with discipline during competition. The moment they begin varying the count or skipping elements in response to emotional state, the routine loses its regulatory anchor function. The value of the routine lies in its predictability. Each repetition reinforces a sense of order and control, reduces cognitive load, and signals to the body that it is time to perform. Over time, this consistent service ritual becomes a reliable platform from which the player can execute with clarity, confidence, and composure, regardless of the pressure of the moment.

After one set all in the Under-16 semi-finals, the super tiebreak had reached 5-5.

Neither player had managed to establish any separation. Every small momentum shift had been immediately answered by the other. As the tiebreak progressed, the quality of the tennis had risen alongside the tension. Rallies became heavier, movement sharper, and the pauses between points noticeably quieter.

Earlier in the afternoon, only a handful of spectators had been watching. But as surrounding matches finished, players, parents, and coaches gradually gathered around the court. By the middle of the tiebreak, several rows of people lined the fences.

Adding another layer of pressure was the winner of the other semi-final. He had arrived courtside carrying a notebook and was sitting quietly beside the fence, intensely recording observations in his Tennis Match Journal. Between points, he scribbled notes about serve patterns, emotional reactions, movement tendencies, and tactical preferences while preparing for whichever opponent he would face in the final the following day.

The player noticed him immediately.

At 5-5, the player prepared to serve.

Throughout the match, his pre-serve bounce routine had varied constantly. Sometimes two bounces. Sometimes four. Once, after a long rally, he had served after only one bounce. To most spectators, it would have appeared insignificant. But his father recognised it immediately as a sign of internal disorganisation.

When calm, the player's serve routine was stable and repeatable. When anxious, it became inconsistent. The very routine that was supposed to regulate him had instead become a symptom of rising pressure.

His coach had addressed this exact issue during training the previous month. The instruction had been simple and completely non-negotiable:

Three bounces. Every time.

Not two.

Not four.

Three.

Regardless of the score. Regardless of momentum. Regardless of how the previous point had unfolded.

At 9-7, standing on match point, he felt the familiar beginnings of a pressure spiral building internally. His chest tightened slightly. Thoughts accelerated. He believed he could win the next point, but the possibilities of failure arrived just as quickly.

What if he shanked the serve?

What if he double-faulted?

What if the match turned from here?

The urge to rush became overwhelming. Part of him wanted to start the point immediately just to escape the discomfort of waiting.

He bounced the ball once and instinctively began the toss. Then he caught himself. He stopped mid-motion and allowed the ball to fall harmlessly back to the court surface.

For a moment, he stood completely still behind the baseline. Then he reset.

He adjusted his grip carefully and began the routine again.

Bounce.

Bounce.

Bounce.

Slow. Even. Exactly three times.

He watched the ball rise and fall against the court surface, allowing the rhythm to steady his breathing. Inhale as the ball rose. Exhale as it dropped. By the third bounce, the urgency inside him had softened slightly. Not disappeared - softened.

He tossed the ball and served.

The serve itself was not spectacular. It drifted safely inside the service line rather than exploding toward the corner. But it landed deep to the opponent's backhand side, starting the rally on neutral terms.

Six shots later, the opponent missed a forehand into the net.

Match.

As the crowd applauded and teammates moved toward the fence, his coach made a mental note of the moment that mattered most - Not the final rally, nor the serve placement...The stopped toss.

The decision, under maximum pressure, to recognise the beginning of the spiral and deliberately return to the routine before it fully took hold.

CHAPTER 13

Fix Socks, Shirt or Clothing: The Controlled Reset Habit

> 💡 **PRACTICAL TIP:** Bending to fix a sock or tucking in your shirt is not about clothing - it is a physical ritual that introduces a moment of stillness, focus, and transition between points.

The adjustment of clothing - pulling up a sock, tucking in a shirt, straightening a sleeve - represents a category of between-point behaviour that shares the same regulatory mechanics as string adjustment or fence tapping, but with one important additional quality: it requires a change in body position. Bending to adjust a sock, for instance, lowers the player's head and changes their visual field, creating a brief moment of physical withdrawal from the upright, court-facing posture of competitive play.

This postural change serves as an additional pattern interrupt. The act of bending, adjusting, and returning to an upright position introduces a micro-transition within the between-point interval - a brief departure from and return to competitive posture that can serve as a physical reset mechanism in its own right.

The Sock Adjustment as an Anchor Habit

Many elite players use clothing adjustments as a consistent between-point habit - not because their socks or clothing are frequently in need of adjustment, but because the action provides a reliable, inconspicuous, and physically grounding ritual that functions consistently across a wide range of emotional and competitive states.

Part of the strength of clothing-adjustment rituals is their consistency across circumstances. Unlike tactical routines, which may change depending on score or situation, a simple sock or shirt adjustment can be performed identically after almost any point. This repeatability helps condition the behaviour into an automatic reset cue over time. Eventually, the action itself begins triggering the psychological state associated with it: slowing down, resetting attention, and returning to composure.

Importantly, the effectiveness of this strategy is not limited to socks alone. Any small, repeatable adjustment to clothing can serve the same regulatory purpose when performed deliberately: straightening a sleeve, adjusting a wristband, pulling down a shirt, repositioning a hat or visor, tightening a shoelace, or brushing clay from the shorts. The specific behaviour matters less than the consistency and intentionality behind it. What these actions share is that they provide a brief, structured interaction with the body and environment that redirects attention away from emotional reactivity and back toward controlled physical process.

The key to maximising the benefit of this habit is, as with all these strategies, intentionality. The player who bends to adjust a sock or clothing item while mentally replaying the previous point derives minimal benefit from the action. The player who bends, focuses completely on the physical sensation of the adjustment of the clothing, and uses the posture change as a moment of genuine withdrawal from the court environment before returning to an upright, ready position - that player has transformed a mundane action into a performance tool.

Nobody watching would have guessed it was intentional. The player had been doing it throughout the entire season - bending down to pull up his right sock after every second or third point, especially after difficult moments in matches. Opponents assumed it was a nervous habit. Parents watching from outside the fence thought the sock genuinely needed constant adjustment or that the elastic had stretched loose from overuse.

Only the coach knew otherwise.

The routine had originally been introduced after two consecutive tournaments earlier in the year where the player had struggled badly between points. He moved too quickly after mistakes, carried frustration visibly into the next rally, and never seemed able to find a reset routine that felt natural or believable to him.

The coach eventually realised the player regulated himself best when the action felt small, physical, and almost invisible. So the inconspicuous sock adjustment came about.

The instruction was simple: after emotionally difficult points, he was to bend down slowly, adjust the right sock deliberately, keep his head lowered briefly, breathe once, then stand and reset.

It looked ordinary enough that nobody paid attention to it. That was part of why it worked.

During the current tournament, he faced the second seed in his age group, a player who had gradually taken control of the match midway through the second set. The opponent was striking the ball cleanly from both wings and had found his range with uncomfortable precision. Returns were landing deep near the baseline. Crosscourt exchanges were pushing the player wider and wider off the court.

As the games passed, his own tennis began speeding up internally. The serve lost reliability first. Then the groundstrokes began flattening and rushing.

By 0-5 in the second set, the momentum felt dangerously close to collapse. After losing the fifth game, he walked slowly toward the back fence and bent down toward his right ankle.

From the outside, it appeared insignificant. Another quick adjustment before the next game.

But he remained there for several seconds longer than usual. Head lowered. Hands against the sock. Breathing slowing.

The position itself created a brief separation from everything happening around him - the scoreboard, the opponent, the spectators beginning to anticipate a quick finish.

For perhaps four seconds, the match paused psychologically.

Then he stood upright again, exhaled slowly, and walked back toward the baseline.

He held serve in the next game. Then won another. Then another and another.

He never recovered the set completely, eventually losing it 4-6. But the downward spiral had been interrupted before it became complete collapse.

The sock adjustment had not suddenly improved his forehand or transformed the quality of his serve. What it provided instead was a small physical interruption at the exact moment he was most vulnerable to emotional acceleration.

The difference between losing the set 0-6 and competing through to 4-6 might have appeared minor on paper. To his coach, it was not minor at all.

Three recovered games represented emotional regulation under pressure. They represented the growing ability to stop momentum swings from becoming emotional avalanches.

In a junior tennis career measured over hundreds of matches, that mattered far more than a single set scoreline.

CHAPTER 14

Tap Your Racquet on the Sole of Your Shoe

💡 **PRACTICAL TIP:** Tapping your racquet on the sole of your shoe - particularly useful on clay courts - is a powerful physical cue that wakes up your feet, refocuses your attention on movement, and reminds you to use your legs.

Why This Works: The Foot-Brain Connection

This strategy may appear unusual at first glance. It is, however, one of the most practically effective between-point reset tools in this collection, and its effectiveness is grounded in solid neurological and biomechanical reasoning.

The feet are the foundation of movement in tennis. Every stroke begins with the feet - with the positioning, the weight transfer, the explosive push-off that generates the kinetic energy transferred up through the body into the racquet. When a player begins to struggle in a match, one of the earliest and most consistent technical breakdowns is in the footwork: steps become shorter, weight transfer less decisive, split steps less pronounced. The player begins to play from static or near-static positions, which reduces every aspect of shot quality and court coverage.

The challenge is that footwork breakdown is often invisible to the player experiencing it. They are focused on the ball, on the opponent, on the score - not on the behaviour of their own feet. The tap of the racquet on the shoe sole creates an immediate, direct physical connection between the racquet and the foot - reminding the player that the foot exists, that it has been tapped, that it should be engaged.

The Mechanics of the Tap

The technique itself is straightforward. Between points - typically after walking to the back fence or during the turn away from the court - the player brings the racquet face down to tap the sole of one shoe. The tap should be firm enough to be felt clearly in the foot, creating a brief tactile and auditory stimulus that registers in the sensory system.

The purpose of the tap is multi-dimensional. First, it physically directs attention to the foot - the sensation of the tap draws the player's awareness downward, toward the part of the body most critical to movement effectiveness. Second, it functions as a self-coaching cue: the tap means 'use your feet.' It is a private reminder, requiring no words and visible only as a brief, unremarkable gesture.

Third - and this is particularly relevant for clay court play, where the technique has the most obvious practical application - the tap can be used to remove clay or dirt that has accumulated on the sole of the shoe during play. Clay on the sole of a shoe reduces grip and creates unpredictable traction. By routinely tapping the sole with the racquet, the player both maintains shoe grip and, as a side effect, builds the habit of attending to their feet as a performance variable.

The Cue as a Reminder to Move Better

The most sophisticated application of this technique is as a deliberate self-coaching cue in the middle of a match. When a player feels their movement becoming passive - when they are arriving at the ball late, when rallies feel like an effortful scramble rather than a controlled positioning exercise - the racquet tap serves as a reminder to recommit to active, anticipatory footwork.

This is the kind of in-match self-correction that, in previous generations of player development, had to wait until a coach's changeover instruction. With the racquet tap as an established cue, the player can deliver this instruction to themselves - privately, immediately, and without any visible disruption to the match.

Body Placement and Positioning Awareness

Beyond footwork specifically, the tap can also function as a broader reminder about body positioning and placement. In tennis, the difference between a shot struck from an optimal position and the same shot struck from a compromised position is often the difference between a winner and an error. Body positioning - getting to the right place, early enough, with the right stance - is the foundation of technical consistency.

When a player uses the racquet tap as a cue for whole-body awareness, they are asking themselves: Am I moving early enough? Am I setting up my position before the ball arrives, or am I arriving at the same time as the ball and improvising? The tap, in this context, is a prompt for the kind of active movement anticipation that separates good technical players from great ones.

The State Clay Court tournament was the event he dreaded every year.

He was a hard-court player by both temperament and upbringing, and the red clay courts at the regional facility seemed to expose every weakness in his game. He had never received formal clay-court training and lacked confidence in both his movement and his ability to slide under control. Footwork that looked instinctive and fluid on hard courts became hesitant on clay.

He planted too early, moved too rigidly, reacted too late.

The extra time clay provided did not help him construct points more effectively. Instead, it created space for doubt and hesitation.

Every year, he struggled for results on the surface. But this tournament mattered. He needed ranking points to maintain his position and hoped to qualify for the National Clay Court tournament draw later in the season.

He had already tried almost every obvious adjustment:

- Technical modifications to his strokes.

- Longer rally tolerance.

- Higher net clearance.

- Different return positions.

- Pre-match warm-up routines specifically designed for clay movement.

None of it fully addressed the central problem that under pressure on clay, his feet stopped simply working properly.

The solution eventually emerged from a conversation with a retired coach who had spent years working with junior players on European clay-court circuits. After watching him train briefly, the coach noticed something immediately: the player's attention under pressure drifted upward toward the ball, the opponent, and the result of the shot, while awareness of his lower body disappeared almost entirely.

The suggestion itself sounded strangely simple.

Every time he walked to the fence between points, he was to tap the sole of his right shoe firmly with his racquet. Not just a light tap, but firm enough to feel the vibration through the shoe and into the bottom of his foot.

The first few times he tried it during practice matches, it felt awkward and slightly artificial. But the sensation itself was unmistakable. The tap created an immediate awareness of his feet and their connection to the court surface.

For the first time in a clay-court match, he became consciously aware of where his weight was positioned before points even began.

During the tournament, midway through a difficult first-round match, he began using the tap consistently between points.

Tap.

Feel the sole.

Feel the ground.

Move.

On the very next point after using it deliberately, something changed.

Instead of waiting passively for the incoming ball, he organised his feet earlier. A small adjustment step happened automatically before the ball crossed the net. His weight settled sooner. The spacing on the shot improved.

The resulting backhand crosscourt landed with a depth and shape he rarely produced on clay. The improvement was not really about the backhand itself. It was the movement beforehand.

For the first time on clay, he was moving actively rather than reactively. The same early footwork patterns he naturally used on hard courts had finally begun appearing on the slower surface.

As the match continued, the racquet tap became a quiet reminder repeated between every point. Not a technical instruction overloaded with detail. Just a physical cue directing attention back toward the foundation of the movement.

Feet first … Then the shot.

The tap did not teach him a new skill. It reminded him, under pressure, to access one he already possessed but had consistently lost on clay when tension rose.

CHAPTER 15

Spin or Twist the Racquet Between Points

> 💡 **PRACTICAL TIP:** A brief spin or twist of the racquet in your hand between points - just a subtle gesture - gives your mind a small, neutral task that interrupts pressure thoughts and restores focus.

The Role of Micro-Tasks in Focus Management

One of the fundamental challenges of managing mental state in a competitive match is the problem of attentional vacancy. Between points, the match pauses but the brain does not. Without a specific focus, the mind naturally returns to the most emotionally charged content available - which is typically the previous point, the scoreline, or concerns about what might happen next. This default is not a character flaw; it is simply the brain operating as it is designed to.

The brain is particularly vulnerable to this process under pressure because emotionally significant events are prioritised by attentional systems designed for survival. Missed opportunities, errors, and perceived threats automatically capture cognitive attention more strongly than neutral events. In a tennis match, this means the mind will often replay mistakes, missed break points, or moments of embarrassment unless it is deliberately directed elsewhere. Effective focus management therefore depends not on trying to suppress thought entirely, but on consistently providing the brain with something more useful to engage with.

Micro-tasks - small, simple, concrete actions that require a minimal but genuine level of attention - provide an alternative destination for this attentional energy. The string adjustment described in Chapter 11 is one such micro-task. The towel wipe described in Chapter 10 is another. The racquet spin or twist introduces a different quality of micro-task: a fluid, dynamic movement that engages the fine motor system of the dominant hand and wrist.

The Mechanics of the Racquet Spin

The racquet spin or twist can take several forms, all of which are effective. The simplest is a single rotation of the racquet around its axis - spinning it so that the face passes through a half or full rotation before being caught and regripped. A slightly more complex version involves a figure-of-eight wrist motion that twists the racquet without full rotation. Both require a level of hand-eye coordination and wrist control that is sufficient to occupy attention without being demanding enough to cause strain or fatigue.

The important quality of this technique is its subtlety. Unlike some between-point gestures that might attract attention from opponents or officials, a quiet racquet spin or wrist twist is essentially invisible. It looks like nothing more than a player casually handling their racquet - which is exactly what it should look like from the outside, while functioning as a deliberate attention management strategy on the inside.

The unobtrusive nature of the racquet spin is psychologically valuable because it allows the player to regulate themselves without creating additional self-consciousness. Large or dramatic between-point behaviours can sometimes increase a player's awareness of their own emotional state or create concern about how they appear to opponents, coaches, or spectators. A small, quiet movement avoids this problem. It integrates naturally into the rhythm of play, allowing regulation to occur privately and efficiently without drawing additional cognitive attention toward the act itself.

Refocusing on the Present Through the Body

The racquet spin works, at its most fundamental level, through the same mechanism as all tactile and proprioceptive reset strategies described in this book: it redirects attention from abstract cognitive content (thoughts about the past or future) to immediate physical experience (the sensation of the racquet moving in the hand, the balance required to control the spin, the moment of catch before regripping).

This redirection is temporary - the mind will return to its previous content if not given a subsequent series of engaging tasks. But temporary is enough. The goal of any between-point strategy is not to eliminate competitive thoughts permanently. It is to create a brief window of regulated attention that allows the player to approach the next point from a slightly less reactive, more neutral state.

The racquet spin is an ideal companion to the other strategies in this book. It can follow the fence tap, complement the string adjustment, or precede the ball bounce routine - slotting naturally into the existing architecture of a between-point routine without requiring significant time or disrupting the flow of the match.

At the age of eleven, after watching far too many Australian Open highlight reels, he developed a habit that quickly irritated his coach.

Between points, while waiting for opponents to prepare or retrieve balls, he would instinctively spin the racquet loosely through his fingers. Sometimes it rotated once. Sometimes twice. He barely seemed aware he was doing it. It simply occupied his hands while time passed between rallies.

His coach noticed immediately and repeatedly kept correcting him during squad sessions.

'You're there to play, not perform circus tricks.'

'You're not a clown, so stop clowning around.'

'Stop playing with the racquet. It's unprofessional.'

Eventually, the player forced himself to stop. The racquet stayed still between points. No spinning. No fidgeting. No unnecessary movement.

Over the following four months, something unexpected happened – his results declined sharply. He was now losing more than he was winning. Matches that he previously managed comfortably became emotional battles his frustration and anger skyrocketed. Minor setbacks escalated into mental spirals that seemed disproportionate to the actual tennis being played.

The confusing part was that his strokes themselves had not deteriorated dramatically. Technically, he was still competing reasonably well, but mentally, he seemed increasingly unstable between points. Neither he nor his parents fully understood why or could work out why.

Concerned by the sudden shift, his parents eventually sought out another coach, one with a sports psychology background who had previously worked extensively with junior players on the European circuit. During the player's first squad session and first private lesson with the new coach, the coach spent most of the time simply observing.

Then, almost unexpectedly, the coach said something unusual, 'I want you to undo everything that changed before the results dropped. Forget the past few months entirely.'

Together, coach and player began tracing backwards through routines, habits, behaviours, and small adjustments that had disappeared around the same time the emotional struggles had started. Eventually, they arrived at the racquet spin.

Instead of discouraging it, the new coach encouraged it immediately. He explained that many athletes develop small physical "ticks" that instinctively help regulate attention and emotional state under pressure. The movement itself was not necessarily the issue. The problem was whether it was being used consciously or unconsciously.

The coach made only one adjustment to the habit: 'Do it deliberately now,' he explained. 'Not because you're bored, but because you're choosing to redirect your attention for two seconds.'

The player found the distinction puzzling at first. What was the difference between doing something absent-mindedly and doing the same thing consciously, when technically it's the same action? How could the same physical action produce a different result simply because of intention?

The coach explained it through an analogy.

'If you scratch your head because it itches, you get temporary relief from the itch. If you deliberately choose to press a specific point on your scalp because it produces a particular sensation that you use to anchor your attention, you get a much more reliable and purposeful result from the same physical action.'

The player understood the difference more clearly once they practised it on court. When he spun the racquet deliberately, paying attention to the sensation of the handle rotating through his fingers, the timing of the catch, the feeling of the regrip, he noticed something important – that for those brief two seconds he genuinely stopped thinking about the previous point. His attention shifted fully into the physical sensation itself.

When the spin happened absent-mindedly, however, his thoughts remained stuck on mistakes, frustration, or outcomes while his hand simply moved automatically in the background. That distinction changed everything.

Over the following tournaments, the racquet spin quietly returned to his between-point routine. But now it carried intention. Each time an opponent delayed between points, bounced the ball excessively before serving, or slowed the pace of play, the player used the additional time differently.

Instead of standing there becoming irritated, he spun the racquet deliberately and attentively.

Spin – Catch – Regrip - Reset

Gradually, his composure returned and the emotional spikes during matches softened. His focus between points became steadier and more controlled. After one tournament, he told his coach that he had barely noticed his opponent's time-wasting or on-court antics because he had been too occupied with the racquet to pay attention to it.

PART THREE

GROUNDING TECHNIQUES

When the mind races ahead to consequences or back to mistakes, the body is always in the present. Grounding techniques bring the athlete back into their body - back to this point, this court, this moment. The six strategies in this section use physical sensation as an anchor for focus.

CHAPTER 16

Press Toes into Shoes

> 💡 **PRACTICAL TIP:** Before every point, press your toes firmly into the front of your shoes and hold for two seconds. This grounds you physically and instantly draws attention back to your body.

The connection between mental state and physical sensation is bidirectional. Just as anxiety can manifest as muscle tension, shallow breathing, or restlessness, deliberately altering physical sensation can interrupt - and often down-regulate - the anxious mind. Grounding techniques are built on this principle. Rather than trying to "think your way" out of pressure, they provide a direct pathway back into the body, where attention can be stabilised and regulated. In fast-paced, high-pressure sports like tennis, this body-first approach is often more reliable than purely cognitive strategies, because it bypasses the very mental loops that tend to escalate under stress.

Pressing the toes firmly into the front of the shoes is one of the most immediate and accessible grounding techniques available on a tennis court. It requires no equipment beyond what the player is already wearing. It takes only a second or two. It is invisible to spectators and opponents. And it produces a clear, unmistakable physical sensation that is difficult for the mind to ignore - which is precisely why it is effective. In moments where attention is scattered or hijacked by emotion, the simplicity and directness of this cue make it highly practical. It gives the player something concrete to do, rather than something abstract to think about.

The Neurological Basis of Toe Pressure

The soles of the feet and the toes contain a high density of sensory nerve endings. These receptors form part of the proprioceptive system - the body's internal monitoring network for position, pressure, and movement. When the toes are pressed firmly against the front of the shoe, a strong proprioceptive signal is generated and transmitted to the brain, particularly to the somatosensory cortex, which processes bodily sensation.

This sensory input competes, in a very real sense, with cognitive noise. The brain has limited attentional bandwidth, and when a clear, novel physical signal is introduced, it naturally draws focus away from abstract thought - such as replaying errors, worrying about outcomes, or anticipating future points. The result is a brief but valuable shift into present-moment awareness. That window may only last a few seconds, but it is often enough. Within that window, the player can insert a slow breath, relax the shoulders, or reinforce a simple tactical cue. Over time, this pairing - physical grounding followed by intentional action - becomes conditioned, strengthening the player's ability to reset efficiently under pressure.

Stability, Balance, and Athletic Readiness

Beyond its neurological grounding effect, toe pressure also serves an important biomechanical function. Pressing the toes into the shoe activates the intrinsic muscles of the foot and engages the lower kinetic chain. This increases proprioceptive feedback from the ground, enhancing balance and postural stability. In practical terms, it helps the player feel more "connected" to the court surface - a subtle but important factor in readiness.

This activation directly supports movement efficiency. A player who is grounded through the feet is better prepared to execute a balanced split step, react quickly to incoming shots, and change direction with control. The action of pressing the toes is small, but it primes the body for the explosive, reactive movements that define tennis. In this way, the technique bridges mental and physical preparation: it calms the mind while simultaneously readying the body.

Applied Context and Parallels in Other Domains

The use of subtle physical cues to maintain alertness and control is not unique to tennis. In military and high-discipline environments, similar strategies are often employed, though not always formally documented in academic literature. Anecdotally, soldiers standing for prolonged periods - such as during guard duty or ceremonial positions - are taught to make small, discreet adjustments within their boots, including shifting weight or pressing the toes, to maintain circulation, alertness, and awareness without breaking posture. While specific peer-reviewed studies on "toe pressing" in soldiers are limited, broader research in human factors and military performance supports the use of micro-movements and proprioceptive engagement to sustain attention and prevent cognitive drift during extended periods of stillness.

Related findings can be seen in studies on vigilance and posture, where even minimal physical engagement - subtle muscle activation, weight redistribution, or tactile feedback - has been shown to help maintain alertness compared to complete immobility. Similarly, research in occupational ergonomics and sports science highlights that light muscular activation can support both circulation and neural arousal, reducing the likelihood of mental fatigue. These principles align closely with the toe-pressing technique: small, controlled physical inputs can stabilise both body and mind.

The combination of neurological grounding and biomechanical activation makes toe pressing a uniquely efficient tool.

It is simultaneously a mindfulness practice, a focus anchor, and a movement preparation strategy - all embedded within a two-second action that requires nothing except awareness and intent. In a match environment where time between points is limited and emotional swings are constant, having such a simple, repeatable intervention can make a meaningful difference. Over time, it becomes part of the player's automatic reset system - a quiet but powerful habit that supports composure, clarity, and readiness on every point.

The match had gone to a third set, and the third set had gone to a tiebreak.

Both players had already spent more than two hours competing in heavy heat and humidity, yet the quality of tennis remained remarkably high. Long baseline exchanges continued deep into rallies, neither player willing to concede ground physically or emotionally. Spectators gathered around the fence had stopped talking almost entirely between points. The tension itself seemed to quiet the court.

The player was known for the consistency of his groundstrokes. What his coach had been working to develop more carefully, however, was his ability to maintain physical composure when pressure rose sharply. Under ordinary match conditions, his footwork was excellent - light, reactive, and organised early.

In the tiebreak, though, his feet had gradually become almost stationary. Not obviously frozen to spectators, but subtly slower. The adjustment steps disappeared first. Then the early preparation. He began reacting after the ball instead of before it. His strokes still looked technically sound, but the movement beneath them had started collapsing under tension.

His coach had prepared for this exact scenario months earlier by introducing something they called the toe-press cue, for the moments when the match had reached a phase of such intensity that the body's natural tendency was to freeze rather than flow. Before each point, the player simply pressed his toes firmly into the front of his shoes. He could feel the resistance clearly. He held it for a count of two.

The sensation was grounding in the most literal sense. He became aware of his feet - their position, their weight distribution, the contact between his shoes and the court surface. He became aware that he was standing on solid ground, that his body was stable, that he was physically ready to move.

It was a such a simple cue. Although not visible to the opponent or anyone else, the effect it had internally was immediate.

Each press redirected his attention downward into his feet and lower body. He became aware of the pressure beneath the balls of his feet, the distribution of his weight, and the connection between his shoes and the court surface. The sensation grounded him in the most literal sense possible.

He stopped feeling like a floating collection of anxious thoughts and started feeling physically connected to the court again.

On match point to the opponent, he stepped in to receive a serve. Before the opponent began the service motion, he pressed his toes firmly into his shoes once more. He felt the tension in his calves soften slightly as his weight settled forward into an athletic stance.

The serve came hard into the backhand corner, dragging him wide immediately. Within seconds, he found himself fully stretched in a defensive position several metres beyond the doubles sideline, scrambling to retrieve a heavy angled forehand.

But this time, his feet were moving. Not perfectly. Not effortlessly. But actively and early. The toe press had brought his attention back to the foundation underneath everything else. And because his attention returned to his feet, his movement patterns followed.

He reached the ball and redirected a deep backhand crosscourt with more shape and depth than the opponent expected from such a defensive position. A lifeline to enable the rally to continue.

A few shots later, the opponent attempted to finish the point early, expecting another defensive reply. Instead, the opponent mistimed the next forehand and drove it long beyond the baseline.

The player turned quietly toward the back fence, breathing heavily, pressing his toes as he too each step. Then came another point, and another. Finally, he got the win in the end, feeling the ground completely present beneath him.

CHAPTER 17

Feel Your Feet on the Ground

> 💡 **PRACTICAL TIP:** Pause before the next point and simply feel the contact between the soles of your shoes and the court surface. This five-second practice returns your attention to the present moment.

Awareness of foot contact with the ground is one of the oldest and most widely used mindfulness practices in clinical and performance psychology. Its appeal lies in its simplicity and its universality: every human being, on every court or field or stage, is always in contact with the ground. That contact is always available as a focus anchor, regardless of what is happening in the mind or in the environment. In high-performance sport, where conditions are constantly changing and external control is limited, this ever-present point of contact becomes a reliable internal reference - something stable the athlete can return to point after point.

In a tennis context, the deliberate awareness of foot-ground contact functions as a reset anchor at a deeper level than many of the more active techniques described in this book. Where string adjustment or racquet movement requires physical engagement, feeling the feet requires nothing more than stillness and attention. It can be accessed instantly - standing at the baseline before a return, walking between points, or sitting during a changeover. This makes it particularly valuable in moments where the player feels mentally overloaded or emotionally unsettled, as it provides a low-effort, high-impact way to re-centre.

The Difference Between Standing and Feeling

Most players stand on the court throughout a match. Very few deliberately feel the ground beneath them. The distinction is significant. Standing is passive - the body's weight is transferred to the ground through the legs, but this occurs automatically, requiring no conscious attention. Feeling the ground is active - the player deliberately directs awareness to the sensory information available from the foot-ground interface, attending to the pressure distribution across the toes, the ball of the foot, and the heel; the firmness or give of the surface; and the subtle shifts in balance as the body stabilises itself.

This directed awareness serves as a grounding anchor in the clinical sense - it creates a moment of concrete, sensory-based present-moment experience that interrupts abstract, future-oriented, or past-oriented cognitive processing. In the language of mindfulness practice, it moves the player from "mind mode" - characterised by thinking, planning, and evaluating - into "body mode" - characterised by sensing, experiencing, and being present. This shift is not philosophical; it is functional. It reduces cognitive noise and creates the conditions for clearer decision-making and more composed execution.

Grounding through the feet is particularly effective under pressure because it shifts attention toward one of the most stable and least emotionally charged sensory experiences available to the body. Thoughts about errors, scorelines, opponents, or outcomes are cognitively and emotionally loaded; the sensation of pressure beneath the feet is neutral, immediate, and concrete. By repeatedly returning attention to this neutral sensory input, the player temporarily reduces the influence of emotionally amplified thinking patterns and creates a calmer internal platform from which the next point can be approached.

Awakening the Feet: From Passive Contact to Active Engagement

Beyond simply feeling the feet, players can actively "awaken" this sensory pathway through deliberate, controlled movement - most effectively through subtle stomping or pressing actions. A light but intentional stomp into the court surface, or a firm press downward through the feet, amplifies sensory input and heightens proprioceptive awareness. This is not about force or aggression, but about clarity of signal. The increased pressure stimulates a greater number of sensory receptors in the soles of the feet, sending a stronger message to the brain: *be here, now.*

This action effectively "switches on" the foot-ground connection. Where passive standing produces a low-level background signal, active engagement produces a sharp, attention-grabbing input. In moments where the mind feels scattered, rushed, or emotionally elevated, this stronger signal can cut through mental noise more effectively than subtle awareness alone. It provides an immediate reset point - a physical interruption that brings the player back into the present moment with clarity.

Neural Activation and Focus

From a neurological perspective, this process can be understood as strengthening the pathway between sensory input and attentional control. When the player deliberately activates the feet - through stomping, pressing, or heightened awareness - they are increasing activity in the somatosensory system and reinforcing its connection to attentional networks in the brain. This does not require complex effort; it requires repetition and intention. Over time, the brain learns to associate this physical cue with a shift in state: from distraction to focus, from tension to readiness.

In practical terms, this means that a simple action - pressing the feet into the ground or giving a controlled stomp before a point - can become a reliable trigger for mental clarity. It is not just a grounding technique; it is a state-change mechanism. The player is no longer waiting to "feel ready" - they are actively creating readiness through physical engagement.

Integration with Movement and Performance

Importantly, awakening the feet is not separate from performance - it enhances it. A player who is connected to the ground through active foot awareness is better positioned to move efficiently. Balance improves, weight transfer becomes more controlled, and the timing of the split step becomes more precise. The same sensory awareness that calms the mind also sharpens the body's readiness to react.

This dual effect - calming and activating simultaneously - is what makes foot-ground awareness such a powerful tool. It is not purely a relaxation technique, nor purely a performance cue; it is both. In the space of a few seconds, the player can stabilise their internal state and prepare their body for action.

Over time, this practice evolves into a subtle but powerful habit. Before key points, after errors, or during moments of rising pressure, the player returns to the same simple process: feel the ground, press into it, awaken the feet. In doing so, they reconnect with the present moment, re-establish control, and step into the next point with clarity, balance, and intent.

★ REAL-LIFE EXAMPLE ★

The changeover came at the worst possible time. Down 1-4 in the second set, having fought back from 0-3 only to drop the serve again, he sat in the player's chair and stared at the ground between his feet. This felt like the most impossible match of his life.

The coach was not permitted to speak to him during the changeover - tournament rules prohibited coaching - but they had prepared for this specific scenario in practice. They had talked about what to do when you were sitting in the chair and the match felt out of reach and the legs were tired and the mind was full of the same thought on a loop: "I'm going to lose this", and "I can't do this".

What they had agreed on was this: feel your feet.

The player looked at his shoes. He pressed the soles against the court surface then giving each foot three distinct stomps - feeling the texture of the hard court through the rubber of his shoe. He became aware of the weight of his legs, the contact of his thighs against the chair, the solid ground beneath his feet. He was here. The court was here. The match was not over.

He had to 'wake his feet'. He had to be present in the point and he had to move to get to his positions to follow his Game Plan and pattern of play. His footwork mattered and he had to remember it. The body and the swing would follow if he got to where he needed to be. The next game went against him. But the one after that he won. And the one after that.

He managed to win overall that day. In his Tennis Match Journal reflection notes, he noted that he had to keep reverting to the basics – grounding himself and remembering to move his feet. His side of the court was his space, and the only way he could perform his best was to be the position he needed to be.

The coach told him afterwards that what he had seen on that changeover - the stillness, the apparent groundedness - was the most significant development of the season. Not the forehand that had improved. Not the serve that was more consistent. The ability to find solid ground beneath him, literally and metaphorically, in the middle of a match he was losing. That was the beginning of something that scorebooks could not capture.

CHAPTER 18

Slight Knee Bend and Reset Stance

> 💡 PRACTICAL TIP: Before returning to the baseline, check your stance: are your knees slightly bent, weight on the balls of your feet? This two-second physical reset restores athletic posture and movement readiness.

The athletic ready position in tennis is defined by a specific postural configuration: knees slightly flexed, weight distributed through the balls of the feet, hips hinged and lowered, trunk inclined forward with a neutral spine, shoulders relaxed, and eyes level with the horizon. This position is not arbitrary - it reflects an optimal alignment for force production, balance, and movement efficiency. From an exercise physiology perspective, it places the body in a pre-loaded state, where key muscle groups - particularly the quadriceps, gluteals, calves, and core stabilisers - are engaged at a low level and ready to contract rapidly. The centre of mass is lowered and positioned slightly forward, improving stability and reducing reaction time for the first step in any direction.

In this posture, the ankle joint sits in slight dorsiflexion, allowing the calf–Achilles complex to function like a spring, storing and releasing elastic energy during movement. The hips are engaged through a controlled hinge, activating the posterior chain - glutes and hamstrings - which are essential for powerful lateral push-offs. The trunk remains stable but not rigid, supported by the deep core musculature, including the transverse abdominis and multifidus, which help maintain spinal alignment while allowing fluid rotation. From a physiotherapy standpoint, this alignment reduces unnecessary joint loading and promotes efficient kinetic chain sequencing, meaning that force generated from the ground can be transferred smoothly through the body into the stroke.

Under competitive pressure, this position erodes. Players become upright, rigid, and heel-weighted - a postural configuration that prepares the body for passive standing rather than dynamic movement. The knees straighten, the hips rise, and the centre of mass shifts backward. This reduces the ability to generate force quickly and compromises balance, making the first movement slower and less coordinated. From a neuromuscular perspective, this upright posture reflects a shift toward protective, energy-conserving patterns often associated with the sympathetic stress response. The body is no longer primed for athletic action; it is bracing.

Posture and emotional state influence each other continuously through bidirectional feedback between the body and nervous system. A rigid, upright posture does not merely reflect tension - it can also reinforce it. When the body becomes stiff, shallow-breathed, and heel-weighted, the brain interprets these physical signals as evidence that the situation is threatening or unstable, further amplifying stress activation. Conversely, returning deliberately to an athletic, balanced posture sends the opposite message: the body is prepared, mobile, and capable of action. In this way, the ready position becomes more than a technical stance - it becomes a physiological signal of readiness and control.

This erosion is often gradual and entirely unconscious. The player does not decide to stand less athletically; the body defaults to a more rigid, defensive posture as cognitive load increases and attention narrows. Over time, this subtle shift can significantly impact performance - not just in movement speed, but in shot quality, timing, and recovery between shots. The loss of athletic posture is therefore not a minor technical issue; it is a systemic breakdown in readiness.

The Reset Stance as a Between-Point Intervention

The deliberate reset of stance between points - taking a moment to consciously re-establish the bent-knee, balls-of-feet athletic position - directly counteracts this default. It serves simultaneously as a physical correction and a psychological cue. Physically, it restores the biomechanical prerequisites for efficient movement: joint angles are re-established, muscle groups are re-engaged, and the centre of mass is repositioned for balance and explosiveness. Psychologically, it reinforces a mindset of readiness and intent: *I am prepared, I am capable, I am ready to compete.*

From a motor control perspective, this reset also reactivates the neuromuscular patterns associated with movement efficiency. By consciously returning to the ready position, the player is effectively "re-priming" the nervous system - reminding the body of the posture from which optimal movement originates. This is particularly important late in matches, when fatigue can further degrade posture and coordination. A consistent reset routine helps maintain movement quality even under physical and mental strain.

The deliberate nature of the reset is critical. A passive return to the baseline without attention to stance will not produce the same benefit as a conscious check and correction. The player should approach the stance reset as a brief but intentional act: check the knee flexion, ensure the hips are slightly hinged rather than upright, feel the weight shift forward onto the balls of the feet, and sense the engagement of the lower body. The shoulders should remain relaxed, avoiding unnecessary tension in the upper body, while the core provides quiet stability.

Over time, this simple intervention becomes a powerful habit loop. Each between-point reset reinforces both posture and mindset, creating a consistent link between physical readiness and mental composure. The player is no longer drifting into position; they are arriving there with purpose. In a sport where fractions of a second and small positional advantages determine outcomes, the ability to repeatedly restore an optimal athletic stance is not just beneficial - it is foundational to sustained high-level performance.

★ REAL-LIFE EXAMPLE ★

The coach had spent the entire day watching matches across the tournament courts and had noticed the same pattern repeating itself over and over again.

Junior players began matches looking athletic and physically engaged - knees bent, weight forward, feet active beneath them. But by the end of long first sets and deep into second sets, the postures gradually changed. Players became more upright. The knees straightened.

Feet flattened against the court. Movement became reactive instead of proactive.

It was almost universal across all competitors. It wasn't laziness or poor fitness alone, rather the visible physical expression of accumulated pressure, fatigue, and mental overload.

In this particular match, the deterioration had started surprisingly early. By midway through the first set, the player's stance had already begun rising higher between shots. By the second set, he was playing most groundstrokes from an almost standing position, knees barely flexed and weight drifting backward toward his heels.

Technically, the strokes themselves remained relatively sound. He was not spraying unforced errors everywhere or losing control of the ball completely. But the movement surrounding the shots had deteriorated noticeably. Balls he normally tracked down comfortably were now passing beyond his reach. His recovery steps became slower and his court coverage shrank point by point. Eventually, he lost the main-draw match and dropped into the consolation draw.

Before the start of his first consolation match, the coach gave him only one instruction: 'Bent knees. Stay low.'

The player found the instruction initially difficult to implement consistently. The bent knee check felt like an additional thing to remember in an environment that was already cognitively demanding. But his coach had anticipated this. 'You don't have to remember it every point,' he had said. 'Start by doing it after every error. Just after errors. Then the habit will spread naturally.'

The errors in the consolation match were followed by a stance check. Bent knees, weight forward. The next point would begin from a better position. Over the course of the match, this correction happened multiple times. Each time, the point that followed the correction was played with measurably better court coverage.

The routine had started. After every missed shot, every rushed error, the player performed a quick stance reset immediately afterwards. He bent his knees, weight forward, lowered his centre of gravity and then resumed play.

As the match progressed, the pattern repeated itself multiple times. Each time he consciously reset his posture after an error, the following point was played with noticeably improved movement. He reached wider balls earlier. Recovery steps became cleaner. Defensively, he covered the court with far greater efficiency.

The tennis itself did not suddenly become spectacular, however the physical platform underneath it stabilised. By the end of the consolation draw event, he had won every remaining match. On his debrief in his Match Journal and in conversations with his coach, he barely noted the actual shot-making and tactical methods he used. Instead, he highlighted something much simpler to fix - the stance.

The player had not transformed his forehand or discovered a new tactical pattern over the course of the tournament. He had simply rebuilt the physical position from which the rest of his tennis operated.

Bent knees, stay low.

Everything else had followed on from there.

CHAPTER 19

Bounce Lightly on Your Toes

> 💡 **PRACTICAL TIP:** A few light bounces on your toes before each point activates the lower body, maintains physical alertness, and physically prevents the static freeze that pressure causes.

Light bouncing on the toes is a technique that operates at the intersection of physical preparation and psychological regulation. Its primary function is biomechanical - maintaining the lower body in an activated, ready state - but its secondary effects on attention and arousal make it a valuable psychological tool as well. It keeps the athlete from becoming static, preserves a sense of fluid readiness, and creates a subtle rhythm that bridges stillness and explosive movement. In high-pressure situations, this gentle, continuous motion prevents the body from "locking up," allowing the player to remain responsive rather than reactive.

From an exercise physiology perspective, the light bounce engages the stretch-shortening cycle (SSC) of the lower limbs - a fundamental mechanism in athletic movement. Each small bounce involves a rapid pre-stretch of the calf muscles (gastrocnemius and soleus) and Achilles tendon, followed by a quick recoil. This cyclical loading and unloading primes the neuromuscular system for explosive action, enhancing the speed and efficiency of subsequent movements such as the split step and first directional push-off. Importantly, the intensity remains low enough to avoid fatigue, functioning instead as a "readiness primer" rather than an energy drain.

At the level of the nervous system, toe bouncing plays a role in regulating activation states through its influence on the autonomic nervous system - particularly the balance between the sympathetic (fight-or-flight) and parasympathetic (rest-and-regulate) branches. Under competitive stress, the sympathetic nervous system tends to dominate, increasing heart rate, muscle tension, and overall arousal. While some degree of this activation is necessary for performance, excessive sympathetic dominance can lead to tightness, rushed decision-making, and impaired coordination.

Light, controlled bouncing provides a form of *regulated activation*. Rather than attempting to suppress arousal, it channels it. The rhythmic, repetitive nature of the movement introduces a degree of predictability and control, which can help stabilise neural activity. In contrast to erratic or forceful movements that amplify sympathetic output, a smooth and consistent bounce can help maintain an optimal level of arousal - keeping the athlete alert without tipping into over-activation. There is also evidence in motor control research that rhythmic movement can support neural synchronisation, improving timing, coordination, and attentional stability.

The physiology of the light bounce is closely related to the split step: the brief, upward jump performed at the moment of the opponent's ball contact that allows the tennis player to change direction quickly in either direction. Both the split step and the between-point bounce activate the same lower-body muscular system and rely on the same pattern of rapid neuromuscular engagement followed by dynamic response. The key difference is that the between-point bounce acts as a preparatory phase - maintaining readiness so that the transition into the split step is seamless rather than delayed.

Rhythm and Activation Regulation

Beyond its physical function, the rhythm of toe bouncing has a direct effect on arousal level. Rapid, heavy bouncing reflects and reinforces high arousal - it is the behaviour of an excited, often over-stimulated player. The contact with the ground becomes louder, the movements less controlled, and the overall tempo increases. This, in turn, feeds back into the nervous system, further elevating sympathetic activation.

Light, rhythmic bouncing at a moderate pace reflects and reinforces a state of calm readiness - alert, prepared, but composed. The movements are quiet, elastic, and controlled.

This type of rhythm acts almost like a metronome for the body, guiding both physical timing and internal tempo. By consciously adjusting the quality of the bounce - softer, lighter, more even - the player sends a signal to the nervous system that control has been re-established.

The relationship between rhythm and activation is well established in both neuroscience and sport performance research. Human physiology naturally entrains to repeated rhythmic input - heart rate, breathing patterns, muscular tension, and attentional tempo all tend to synchronise with the pace of repetitive movement. This is why rushed, erratic movement often increases feelings of chaos and tension, while smooth and controlled rhythm tends to stabilise the nervous system. In tennis, the bounce rhythm therefore becomes more than preparation for movement; it becomes a subtle method of regulating the player's overall internal tempo.

By deliberately managing this rhythm, the player gains a practical tool for fine-tuning arousal levels in real time. For players who tend toward over-excitement on important points, slowing and softening the bounce can help bring activation back into an optimal range. For players who feel flat or under-stimulated, slightly increasing the energy of the bounce can elevate readiness. In this way, the bounce becomes more than a habit - it becomes a dial the player can adjust to regulate their internal state.

Over time, consistent use of this technique builds a strong association between movement rhythm and mental state. The player learns not only to recognise when they are too tense or too flat, but to actively correct it through a simple, repeatable physical cue. In a sport where milliseconds matter and composure is constantly tested, this ability to self-regulate through movement provides a subtle yet powerful competitive edge.

The player first noticed it while watching a junior national-level competitor several years older than him compete at a major tournament.

The older player had already travelled internationally for junior ITF events and carried himself differently to most players his age. Between points, there was a constant subtle movement to him - a light bounce through the feet and ankles that never fully stopped. Even while standing still, he appeared physically alive in a way that most junior players did not. It made him look powerful, dangerous and intimidating on court.

The younger player watched for nearly an entire set before eventually asking the older player's father about it while they stood near the side fence. The father had smiled immediately, as though he had been asked the question many times before. 'He stays on his toes between points,' he explained. 'It stops the body from freezing under pressure.'

In his next practice session, he experimented with the movement himself. Between rallies, instead of standing flat-footed behind the baseline, he bounced lightly through the balls of his feet in a small rhythmic motion. Initially, it felt surprisingly difficult. Not technically difficult - physically demanding. The constant activation required more attention and energy than he was used to sustaining between points. After twenty minutes, his calves were burning lightly and the movement still felt unnatural.

By the second training session, the bounce has already started becoming more automatic, and he noticed a corresponding improvement in his movement quality from the very first step of each rally. His reaction time improved and he split-step more naturally. He also felt his recovery movement were quicker and lighter.

At his next tournament, the bounce became even more valuable. The event was played in brutal heat, with temperatures climbing throughout the afternoon until the courts themselves radiated visible waves of heat upward into the air. Both players began showing the normal physical signs of thermal fatigue as the match progressed. Shoulders slumped slightly between points. Walks to the towel became slower. The natural instinct under those conditions was to conserve movement wherever possible.

The player understood that risk and conscientiously decided to maintain the bounce deliberately, even during the rest periods between points. His thoughts repeated 'Light feet. Stay alive.'

Across the net, his opponent who was normally an excellent mover had gradually become more static as the heat and fatigue accumulated. He began waiting flat-footed for balls rather than initiating movement early, and his recovery steps shortened. The explosive first movement into wide balls started disappearing.

The contrast between the two players grew more obvious with each passing game. By the final set, the player was consistently reaching balls that his opponent no longer could. Not because he possessed superior athletic ability overall, but because each point began from a different physical state.

One body had gradually shut down under fatigue, the other had stayed active by deliberate choice.

He took the win and on his debrief in his Tennis Match Journal logbook, he reflected that it was the most physically consistent performance he had in those conditions.

CHAPTER 20

Stand Tall, Chest Up

> 💡 PRACTICAL TIP: Between points, consciously lift your chest and stand tall. This simple postural change signals confidence to your brain, your opponent, and your own nervous system simultaneously.

The relationship between posture and psychological state is one of the most practically significant findings in embodied cognition research. The traditional view holds that emotional state drives posture: we slump when we are defeated, stand tall when we are confident. But research over the past two decades has established that the relationship is bidirectional: posture also drives emotional state.

When a player consciously adopts an upright, chest-open posture - regardless of how they feel in that moment - measurable changes occur in both physiology and psychology. Breathing deepens naturally as the ribcage expands, improving oxygen exchange and reducing the shallow, rapid breathing associated with anxiety. There is also evidence suggesting subtle shifts in neuroendocrine response, including reductions in stress-related hormones and small increases in those associated with confidence and assertiveness. More importantly for performance, the player's *perceived* sense of control and capability improves. This perception is critical: in competitive environments, confidence is not simply a reflection of past success - it is an active state that can be influenced and reinforced through physical behaviour.

Over time, repeatedly adopting this posture in moments of pressure conditions the brain to associate the physical stance with a state of readiness and composure. The body becomes a trigger for the mind. Even when confidence is low, the act of standing tall interrupts the downward spiral of negative self-perception and replaces it with a more stable, performance-oriented state. This is not superficial; it is a practical method of regulating internal experience through external action.

The Public Dimension: What the Opponent Sees

Standing tall between points also has a tactical dimension that extends beyond the player's own internal state. Tennis is not played in isolation - it is an interactive contest where both players are constantly reading and interpreting cues. Body language is one of the most immediate and influential of those cues. An opponent is not just responding to the ball; they are responding to perceived confidence, energy, and emotional stability.

A player whose posture becomes progressively more defeated - shoulders rounding, head lowering, movement slowing - communicates vulnerability. This signal, whether conscious or not, can alter the opponent's mindset. It may encourage them to play more aggressively, take greater risks, or feel a sense of control over the match. In contrast, a player who maintains an upright, composed, and consistent physical presence - even when making errors or falling behind - removes that signal. They present as stable, unaffected, and difficult to read.

This creates a subtle but important psychological effect. When an opponent cannot detect weakness, uncertainty begins to emerge. Questions form: *Are they really struggling? Are they about to lift? Am I actually in control here?* This uncertainty can disrupt the opponent's own confidence and decision-making. In this way, posture becomes part of the competitive exchange - not through deception, but through disciplined self-presentation.

Projecting an unshakeable demeanour does not mean exaggeration or theatrics. In fact, the most effective presence is often understated. Consistent posture, steady movement, neutral or focused facial expression, and controlled pacing between points all contribute to an impression of composure. This consistency is what matters. If posture fluctuates dramatically with the scoreline, the signal becomes unreliable. If it remains stable, it becomes credible.

Importantly, this outward projection feeds back into internal confidence. When a player behaves *as if* they are composed and in control, the brain begins to align with that behaviour. This is a form of behavioural reinforcement: action precedes feeling. The player is not waiting to feel confident before standing tall - they are using posture to *create* confidence.

At higher levels of competition, where technical and physical differences between players are often minimal, these psychological edges become decisive. The player who can maintain a consistent, confident physical presence - regardless of momentum swings - not only improves their own internal state but also shapes the emotional landscape of the match. They become harder to break down, harder to read, and harder to play against.

Ultimately, posture is more than appearance. It is communication - both inward and outward. It tells the body how to feel, and it tells the opponent what to believe. The player who understands and applies this consistently develops a quiet but powerful advantage: they look composed, they feel more composed, and they compete with a level of stability that others struggle to disrupt.

Down 2-5 in the second set after losing the first set 4-6, the physical weight of the match had started showing clearly in the player's body.

His shoulders had rounded forward noticeably. His head sat lower between points than it normally did. Even the way he walked had changed - a slight forward lean through the upper body that his father immediately recognised from previous difficult matches. It was the posture he adopted when he had emotionally started believing the match was already gone.

Watching quietly from the stands, his mother leaned slightly toward his coach and said: 'Look at his chest.' She was right, his chest posture had collapsed inward into the unmistakable physical signature of a player mentally shrinking before the scoreboard had officially confirmed defeat.

They could not coach him from the stands however needed to get a message to him to fix himself. His coach had discussed this exact situation repeatedly during private lessons before, always harping on about 'standing up', 'lifting his chest up, loud and proud'.

The player sat heavily in the chair and glanced briefly toward his cheer squad, with the exhausted whingy expression of someone already anticipating defeat. What caught his attention immediately, though, was the way both of them were sitting. His mother and coach were sitting there, perfectly upright, almost unnaturally upright. It looked as though they each had a pole up their you-know-what.

The message was obvious without a single word being spoken. Suddenly, he became aware of his own posture – his rounded shoulders and collapsed chest and the compressed breathing he didn't realise he was doing.

Slowly, he straightened. He rolled the shoulders back slightly and lifted the chest upward. At first, the movement felt awkward and strangely artificial in the middle of a match that seemed to be slipping away from him.

Almost immediately he noticed that his breathing deepened. The lifted chest created space his collapsed posture had been restricting for nearly an entire set. He took one slow breath. Then another. The air moved more freely through his lungs than it had in the previous thirty minutes. He felt optimistic and felt present again.

The next game went on forever. It was the longest game of the match, contested to eleven deuces, and he won it. Eventually he lost the set 5-7 but something important had shifted after that changeover.

From 2-5 onward, he competed with a physical presence that had been missing earlier in the match. The posture change had not magically improved his strokes, but it altered the physical state from which his decisions were being made. Upright posture allowed freer breathing. Freer breathing reduced the sense of panic. Reduced panic improved clarity.

Afterward, during the debrief, his coach pointed out that the quality of his decision-making in the final games had been noticeably better than during the earlier stages of the match when his posture had completely collapsed.

Although standing tall did not save that particular match, it did stop his mental spiral and boosted his confidence. His reflection journal entry noted that he needs to remember to stand tall the *entire* match, not wait until he is on the last set and already starting to lose his marbles. In the long-term development of a junior player, that understanding was far more important than a single match result.

CHAPTER 21

Roll Shoulders Back

> 💡 **PRACTICAL TIP:** Roll your shoulders back and down between points to actively release upper-body tension and re-open the chest. This is the physical reset your body needs after a tense point.

The shoulder roll is a more active version of the shoulder drop described earlier in this book. Where the shoulder drop is a passive release - allowing the elevated shoulders to fall - the shoulder roll is a deliberate circular movement that takes the shoulders through their full range of motion before returning them to a low, relaxed position. This active movement addresses not only the elevation of tension but also the forward rounding that frequently accompanies stress-related shoulder tightening. In doing so, it restores both mobility and alignment across the shoulder girdle, which is critical for efficient stroke production and injury prevention over the course of a match.

Competitive play encourages a specific pattern of shoulder tension: the shoulders move forward and up, reflecting both the physical demands of stroke production and the psychological state of defensive readiness. From a physiotherapy perspective, this position places the scapula (shoulder blade) into protraction and elevation, often accompanied by internal rotation of the humerus (upper arm). Over time, this reduces the available subacromial space in the shoulder joint, potentially limiting overhead range of motion and placing additional strain on structures such as the rotator cuff tendons. It also shifts load away from the larger stabilising muscles of the upper back - including the middle and lower trapezius and rhomboids - and toward smaller, fatigue-prone muscles in the neck and upper shoulders.

Physical education research conducted with junior athletes has consistently demonstrated that the upper trapezius - the muscle that runs from the base of the skull across the top of the shoulders - carries more tension in junior tennis players during tournament competition than in any other comparable youth sport. This finding, while academic in origin, has clear practical implications. It explains why young players, in particular, tend to present with elevated shoulders, shortened neck posture, and visible tightness as matches progress. The upper trapezius becomes overactive as it compensates for both physical fatigue and psychological stress, effectively "holding" tension in response to pressure. Left unaddressed, this not only impacts posture but can interfere with fluid stroke mechanics, particularly in the serve and overhead, where freedom of movement through the shoulder complex is essential.

The shoulder roll directly counteracts this pattern. By moving the shoulders back and down, it encourages scapular retraction and depression - the optimal position for shoulder stability and force transfer. This re-engages the posterior chain of the upper body, particularly the mid-back musculature, which plays a key role in maintaining posture and supporting rotational movements. At the same time, it promotes external rotation of the shoulder joint, improving joint alignment and reducing unnecessary compression.

From an exercise physiology standpoint, this repositioning enhances the efficiency of the kinetic chain, allowing energy generated from the lower body and trunk to transfer more effectively through the shoulders and into the racquet.

The movement also has important effects on the muscles of the chest and arms. Repeated forward rounding under stress leads to tightening of the pectoralis major and minor, as well as the anterior deltoid. This can restrict arm swing, reduce reach, and subtly alter stroke mechanics - particularly on serves and forehands. The shoulder roll acts as a dynamic stretch for these anterior structures, while simultaneously activating the posterior muscles that support a more open, balanced posture. The result is not just reduced tension, but improved movement quality and greater freedom through the hitting arm.

From a nervous system perspective, the shoulder roll introduces a controlled, rhythmic movement that can help regulate neuromuscular tone. Prolonged stress often leads to increased baseline muscle activation - a state where muscles remain partially contracted even at rest, driven by elevated sympathetic nervous system activity. This contributes to stiffness, reduced coordination, and inefficient movement patterns. The slow, deliberate nature of the shoulder roll provides a signal to the nervous system to reduce this unnecessary activation. By moving through a full, smooth range of motion, the brain receives feedback that it is safe to release excess tension, particularly in the overactive upper trapezius.

The shoulder roll also indirectly influences breathing mechanics, which are commonly disrupted under competitive stress. Elevated and rounded shoulders restrict the movement of the rib cage and encourage shallow, upper-chest breathing patterns dominated by accessory neck muscles. By restoring the shoulders to a lower and more open position, the movement allows the rib cage to expand more freely and supports deeper diaphragmatic breathing. This creates a compounding regulatory effect: as posture improves, breathing efficiency improves, and as breathing settles, overall muscular activation and nervous system tension tend to reduce in parallel.

Additionally, the act of coordinating the movement engages motor control pathways that promote more efficient muscle recruitment patterns. Instead of isolated, reactive contractions - often dominated by the neck and upper shoulders - the body returns to a more integrated pattern, distributing load appropriately across the shoulder girdle and upper back. This has a direct carryover to stroke fluidity, allowing the player to swing more freely and with less restriction, even under pressure.

The Mechanics and Timing of the Shoulder Roll

The shoulder roll is performed by slowly moving the shoulders backward and upward, then continuing the circular motion backward and downward, completing the circle in the back-and-down position - which is the optimal posture for competitive tennis. The movement should be smooth and controlled, rather than rushed, allowing the player to feel each phase of the motion. One rotation in each direction is typically sufficient to reset the shoulder position and reduce accumulated tension.

Attention should be given not only to the shoulders themselves, but to the surrounding structures. The neck should remain relaxed, avoiding compensatory tightening in the upper trapezius. The arms should hang loosely, allowing the movement to originate from the shoulder girdle rather than being forced through the elbows or wrists. The chest should open slightly as the shoulders move back, reinforcing an upright, balanced posture and counteracting the forward collapse that often develops during play.

The ideal timing for the shoulder roll is during the walk to the back fence - a moment when the player is already engaged in purposeful movement and when the action will be least conspicuous. It can also be incorporated into the changeover routine, particularly when combined with other recovery strategies such as controlled breathing or light stretching. In these moments, the shoulder roll becomes part of a broader physical reset, restoring posture, mobility, and neuromuscular balance before the next sequence of points.

Over time, this simple movement becomes more than a corrective exercise - it becomes a cue. A cue to release unnecessary tension, to down-regulate overactive muscle groups such as the upper trapezius, and to re-establish optimal alignment across the upper body. In a sport where small physical restrictions can significantly impact performance, the ability to repeatedly reset the shoulders is a subtle but powerful advantage - supporting both physical efficiency and psychological composure throughout the match.

The player had been competing in tournaments for nearly twelve years and, over the previous eighteen months, had been working closely with a tennis-specialist sports physiotherapist on a recurring issue: upper-body tension during competition.

The problem had not originated entirely on the tennis court. Years of daily study, homework, and computer use (often close to six hours each weekday) had gradually produced a rounded, forward posture through the shoulders and upper back. Under competitive pressure, that posture became even more pronounced. His shoulders crept upward toward his ears, chest tightened, and the freedom of his swing slowly disappeared.

The physiotherapist had introduced shoulder rolls originally as a simple daily mobility exercise – simple slow rotations ensuring the full range of motion to release the tension before it accumulated. His coach immediately recognised the competitive value of the movement and eventually incorporated it into the player's between-point routine.

During the semi-final of the seasonal League tournament, he faced the number one seed - a player he had lost to in all five of their previous meetings.

By the third set, the match had reached 4-4. Physically both players were still competing well but internally, the pressure had become obvious. The points stretched longer and the pauses between rallies became louder with the whinging negative self-talk. Every small momentum shift carried more emotional weight than earlier in the match. The player could feel the tension and constriction beginning to return across his upper body. The familiar tightening through the neck, shoulders, and chest that usually appeared shortly before his strokes began breaking down technically under pressure. This time, though, he recognised it early.

As silly as it may have looked, the player deliberately implemented the shoulder roll at every between-point interval from 4-4 onwards. The rolls were slow and deliberate, covering the full range of motion, accompanied by a long exhale. The movement itself looked insignificant to most spectators. But internally, it prevented the tension from accumulating unchecked. The shoulders lowered slightly after each exhale. The chest stayed open. The arms continued moving freely rather than stiffening progressively as the set tightened.

Across the net, the opponent noticed something different too. Having played against him five previous times over several years, he expected the same physical deterioration under pressure that had occurred in earlier matches. But during this match, the player looked different. He appeared more confident and upright, and was more fluid through his contact. The opponent could not fully identify what had changed, simply that he looked like a different player.

The player eventually won 6-4 in the third. After the match, both his coach and league teammates described it as the best he had ever competed under pressure. The shoulder rolls were not the entire reason however they were a part of what allowed the rest of his tennis to function when the pressure became highest.

Because in tightly contested matches, technical breakdown often begins in the body long before it appears in the scoreboard.

PART FOUR

VISUAL FOCUS CUES

Where your eyes go, your mind follows. The five strategies in this section train your visual attention - teaching you to choose deliberately what you look at between and during points, and using that choice to stabilise focus, reduce distraction, and sharpen execution.

CHAPTER 22

Focus on the Centre of the Net Cord

> 💡 **PRACTICAL TIP:** Between points, briefly fix your gaze on the centre of the net cord. This single visual anchor stabilises divided attention and draws you back to the centre of the court and the game.

Visual attention in tennis is a performance asset that most players manage poorly. Under low-pressure conditions, visual attention tends to be well-directed - focused on the ball, the opponent's position, and the relevant court geometry. Under competitive pressure, however, attention fragments. The eyes begin to scan, flicker between multiple objects, drift toward the scoreboard or the watching crowd, or disengage from the external environment altogether as internal dialogue takes over. This fragmentation is not just a mental issue; it has direct consequences for timing, spacing, and decision-making, because perception drives action.

The deliberate fixation of gaze on a single, stable, neutral visual reference - the centre of the net cord - provides an immediate antidote to this fragmentation. The net cord's position at the geometric centre of the court makes it an ideal anchor: it is always visible, always consistent, and inherently connected to the spatial structure of the game. By directing the eyes - and therefore attention - to this point between rallies, the player simplifies the visual environment, reducing cognitive load and re-establishing perceptual clarity before the next point begins.

Why the Net Cord Specifically

The net cord occupies a unique psychological neutrality that makes it more effective as a between-point focal point than alternative objects in the visual field. It is not the opponent (which can trigger comparison, tension, or emotional reactivity), not the ball (which may carry associations from the previous error or success), and not the court lines (which can evoke frustration around line calls). It is a static, featureless point at the centre of the playing geometry - a visual anchor with no emotional charge.

This neutrality is critical. The brain is constantly attaching meaning to what it sees. When attention is directed toward emotionally loaded stimuli, cognitive resources are consumed by interpretation and reaction. By contrast, focusing on a neutral object allows the visual system to remain engaged without triggering additional emotional processing. In effect, it gives the mind a brief reset - a pause from interpretation - while still maintaining external focus.

Near-Far Gaze and Visual Reset

There is growing evidence within vision science and sports performance research that alternating between near and far gaze can support visual efficiency, attentional flexibility, and even reduce ocular fatigue. This concept is often used in clinical and occupational settings (for example, the "20-20-20 rule" for screen use), but it also has relevance in sport. Shifting gaze from a distant point (such as the opponent's baseline or beyond the court) to a nearer, clearly defined object (such as the net cord) requires the visual system to adjust focus (accommodation) and eye alignment (vergence). This brief reset can help "re-centre" the visual system after periods of diffuse or scattered attention.

In a tennis context, this means that bringing the gaze inward to the net cord between points can act as a visual reset before expanding outward again to track the next rally. The eyes move from a potentially unfocused or overstimulated state into a controlled, precise fixation, and then back out into dynamic tracking. This process may also support peripheral awareness. When central gaze is stabilised - fixed calmly on a single point - the surrounding visual field (peripheral vision) often becomes clearer and more accessible. In contrast, when the eyes are darting or over-scanning, both central and peripheral perception can degrade.

Practical Implications: Net Cord vs Distant Targets

Focusing on a distant object - such as a tree beyond the court or a point in the crowd - can have some calming effect, particularly in reducing immediate intensity. However, it lacks the functional relevance and precision of the net cord. A distant gaze tends to promote a more diffuse visual state, which may be useful for relaxation but less effective for preparing the perceptual system for the demands of the next point.

By contrast, the net cord provides a near, sharp, and task-relevant focal point. It aligns the player visually with the court, reinforces spatial awareness, and primes the eyes for the type of tracking required in play - quick, precise, and centred. It also shortens the visual "reset loop": the player does not need to bring their gaze back from outside the playing area, as the focus remains within the competitive environment.

Integration with Performance

The net cord focus should not be prolonged. One to two seconds of deliberate fixation is sufficient. During this time, the player allows the eyes to settle, the visual system to stabilise, and attention to consolidate. This can be paired effectively with a breath, a physical reset cue, or a simple tactical intention.

Over time, this practice conditions a reliable attentional pattern: after each point, the eyes return to a known anchor, the mind resets, and the player prepares again. In a sport where visual clarity under pressure is critical, this small habit can have a disproportionate impact. It restores order to the perceptual system, supports peripheral awareness, and ensures that when the next ball is struck, the player is not just physically ready - but visually and cognitively aligned with the task at hand.

★ REAL-LIFE EXAMPLE ★

The coach had introduced the net-cord focus exercise as part of a broader visual attention training programme developed after reading research on something known as the "quiet eye" - the period of stable gaze fixation that consistently precedes effective motor execution in skilled performers. The research had demonstrated that expert performers in precision sports consistently show a longer and more stable pre-execution gaze fixation than non-expert performers. Essentially under pressure, elite athletes visually settled whilst non-elite athletes visually scattered. The coach had developed training interventions that explicitly develop this skill improve performance under pressure.

The player became one of three junior athletes selected for the programme. From the beginning, his coach noticed that the player's visual behaviour between points lacked stability. His eyes moved constantly - toward the opponent, the crowd, nearby courts, ball marks, scoreboards, parents behind fences. At first, the coach had interpreted this pattern as simply youthful curiosity and alertness before recognising it as a performance liability.

The training intervention itself was remarkably simple. After every point in practice, before beginning any other part of the between-point routine, the player was instructed to visually locate the centre of the net cord and hold his gaze there for a minimum of two seconds.

Nothing more, simply find the centre and look at it, then continue with the routine.

The effect was not immediately apparent in his match results. The coach however measured something else: the time between the end of a point and his first purposeful action - the decision latency that preceded his between-point routine. Before the training, this latency was variable, sometimes extending to four or five seconds of unfocused scanning. After three weeks of net cord fixation practice, the latency had reduced and stabilised. He was making his first decision (the visual anchor) faster and more consistently.

In match conditions, this showed as a general improvement in the quality of his between-point transitions. He appeared - to coaches, opponents, and parents - to be a player who was always in control of himself between points.

The net cord had given his visual system somewhere stable and predictable to go immediately after pressure moments. By repeatedly directing attention toward the same fixed point, he reduced much of the visual and cognitive noise that had previously characterised his between-point behaviour.

CHAPTER 23

Look at Your Strings

> ♀ **PRACTICAL TIP:** Looking at your strings between points is not aimless - it is a deliberate internal focus that separates you from the court environment and gives your mind a momentary sanctuary.

Where the net cord provides an external visual anchor that re-centres attention within the geometry of the court, the next progression is to bring that focus even closer - into the player's own immediate space. This shift from an external, court-based reference to an internal, equipment-based reference deepens the reset. It moves attention from the environment the player is competing *in* to the object they are competing *with*. In doing so, it reinforces both attentional control and a sense of ownership over the moment.

The strings of a tennis racquet are, at one level, simply the tools of the sport. At another level - particularly in the context of between-point attention management - they represent a portable, always-available focal point that is entirely within the player's personal space. Unlike the opponent, the ball, or even the court itself, the racquet carries no external judgement, no scoreline, and no emotional narrative. It is neutral, consistent, and fully controllable. This makes it an ideal anchor when the player needs to briefly disengage from the broader competitive environment.

Looking at the strings is a form of visual narrowing. After using a central court reference like the net cord to stabilise attention, shifting the gaze to the racquet face reduces the visual field further. The eyes move from a mid-distance focal point to a near, highly defined object. This contraction of visual space has a settling effect on attention. It limits incoming visual information, reduces distraction, and allows the perceptual system to "quieten" before the next point. In practical terms, it is a way of stepping out of the match for a moment without physically leaving the court.

Visual attention and emotional intensity are closely linked. Under stress, the eyes tend to scan rapidly between multiple stimuli - the opponent, the crowd, the scoreboard, movement around the court - which increases cognitive load and reinforces a sense of chaos or urgency. Deliberately fixing the gaze on a single stable object interrupts this scanning behaviour. The visual system settles, attentional demands reduce, and the nervous system receives fewer competing inputs to process. In this sense, focusing on the strings is not merely about looking downward; it is about simplifying the player's perceptual world for a few crucial seconds between points.

Over time, this repeated act of narrowing and stabilising visual attention can become a conditioned cue for composure. The moment the player drops their gaze to the strings, the nervous system begins recognising the sequence: slow down, reset, prepare again. What begins as a deliberate attentional strategy gradually becomes an automatic transition into a calmer and more controlled competitive state.

Combining Visual Focus with Physical Inspection

The most effective version of this technique combines visual attention to the strings with the physical string-straightening described in Chapter 11. The player looks at the strings while adjusting them, attending both to their visual alignment and to the tactile feedback of the string under the thumb. This dual sensory engagement - visual and tactile - creates a stronger grounding effect than either channel alone. The eyes focus on a precise, controlled task, while the hands reinforce that focus through touch.

There is also a subtle but important performance benefit to this inspection. By visually checking the string bed - noting alignment, spacing, and any early signs of wear - the player reinforces a sense of equipment awareness and readiness. This contributes to confidence in the racquet's response at contact. The act is not just a reset; it is a micro-calibration. The player is, in effect, confirming: *my tools are in order, and I am prepared to use them.*

From a perceptual standpoint, this near-focus task also complements the earlier use of the net cord. The visual system moves through a controlled sequence - from broader court awareness, to a central external anchor, to a close internal focal point. This progression helps reset both focus and visual acuity. After a brief period of near fixation, the eyes are often better prepared to re-expand outward and pick up the ball cleanly on the next point. The transition is smoother, and the likelihood of visual distraction is reduced.

The integration of looking at the strings with other between-point behaviours creates a consistent and repeatable visual routine. The player turns slightly away from the court, allowing the broader environment to fall out of view. The gaze drops to the racquet face, where attention is anchored through inspection and adjustment. Movement - such as walking to the back fence - can occur while maintaining this inward focus. Only once the reset is complete does the player lift their gaze, returning attention outward in a deliberate and controlled manner.

Over time, this sequence becomes automatic. The eyes follow a familiar path, the mind follows the eyes, and the player re-enters the next point with greater clarity and composure. In a match environment filled with potential distractions, the ability to direct and contain visual attention - first outward to stabilise, then inward to reset - provides a quiet but highly effective layer of control.

The strangest thing about playing the state number-one seed was not the quality of the tennis. It was the feeling of being watched by someone who knew exactly what they were looking for and noticed everything. Every movement he made between points, during changeovers, at his towel, and even on the walk from one end of the court to the other - felt scrutinised in a way that ordinary opponents did not create. Ordinary opponents created pressure through shot-making and winners, this opponent created pressure through presence.

Before his match his coach had warned him about exactly this. 'Elite players read body language very early and very accurately,' he had been told. 'Be conscious of what you show your opponent.' The advice had seemed abstract until this match, where it felt entirely concrete.

The string-looking technique had been in his routine for six months, but he had never previously recognised its tactical dimension. Looking at his strings meant that his eyes were not meeting his opponent's eyes. They were not scanning the opponent for tactical information. They were directed inward, at the racquet, communicating nothing about his internal state to anyone observing.

His opponent, he noticed during the match, tended to look directly at him between points - reading, assessing and studying his every move. The player's inward gaze remained directed downward to his racquet, giving the opponent very little social information to work with. He became, visually, a blank canvas. The opponent was forced to make tactical and emotional assessments without access to the normal information players often extract from body language and eye contact.

Whether this produced a measurable tactical advantage was impossible to prove however throughout the match, the player felt noticeably less exposed than he normally did against high-level opponents.

The player won the match 6-4 7-5, and in the debrief the coach noted that he had managed the social environment of the court - the visibility and social pressure of competing against the top seed - more effectively than in any previous match of comparable importance.

'Where were your eyes when you were at the fence?' the coach asked.

'On my strings'.

'And how did that feel?'

He thought about it for a moment. 'Private,' he said eventually. 'Like no one could see inside.'

CHAPTER 24

Pick a Target Spot Before Serve or Return

> 💡 **PRACTICAL TIP:** Before every serve and every return, identify a specific target. A committed, pre-selected target simplifies the mind, reduces hesitation, and dramatically improves execution.

Decision noise is one of the primary drivers of performance variability under pressure. When a player approaches a serve or return without a clear, pre-committed target, the decision-making process must occur during the execution - while the ball is being struck or, in the case of the serve, during the toss and swing. This real-time decision-making under time pressure is the enemy of clean execution. It fragments attention, disrupts timing, and often results in a compromised swing - neither fully committed nor fully controlled.

Under pressure, indecision rarely appears as complete uncertainty. More often, it appears as partial commitment: the player begins the motion while still mentally debating alternatives. A serve is started toward the backhand corner before a late hesitation shifts intention toward the body serve. A forehand is initiated crosscourt before the player abruptly attempts to redirect it down the line. These last-moment adjustments disrupt the fluid sequencing of the movement and increase muscular tension at precisely the moment relaxation and acceleration are required most.

Pre-point target selection - identifying a specific target before initiating play - eliminates this problem by resolving the decision in advance. By the time the execution begins, the question of where the ball should go has already been answered. The body is then free to commit fully to the movement pattern required to send the ball to that location. This separation of decision and execution is critical: clarity first, action second.

The Cognitive Science of Pre-Commitment

Research in cognitive psychology demonstrates that pre-commitment to a course of action dramatically increases the likelihood of effective execution. In sport, this is often described through the concept of *implementation intention* - the explicit pre-planning of a specific action in response to a specific situation. Under conditions of stress and cognitive load, this approach reduces hesitation and improves behavioural consistency.

For a tennis player, implementation intention translates into clear internal statements such as: *"This serve goes wide to the backhand,"* or *"If the return comes to my forehand, I go heavy crosscourt."* These statements act as mental triggers, linking situation to action. They do not guarantee perfect execution, but they remove indecision from the moment of performance. The mind is no longer negotiating options mid-swing; it is executing a pre-selected plan.

Adding Visualisation: Seeing the Outcome Before it Happens

To strengthen this process further, players can pair target selection with brief, deliberate visualisation. Before initiating the serve or return, the player forms a clear mental image of the ball travelling along the intended path and landing precisely on the chosen target. This image should be simple, specific, and sensory-rich: the trajectory of the ball, the height over the net, the point of contact with the court, and even the sound of the bounce.

This is not imagination for its own sake - it is motor preparation. The brain does not fully distinguish between vividly imagined movement and actual movement. When a player visualises a successful outcome, they are activating many of the same neural pathways involved in executing that action. In effect, they are running a mental rehearsal immediately before the physical one. This primes the motor system, making the intended movement more accessible and more likely to be reproduced accurately.

There is also a psychological component to this process that aligns with broader performance and mindset principles. Visualising a successful outcome - and briefly allowing oneself to *feel* that success as if it has already occurred - reinforces confidence and reduces doubt. Concepts popularised in works such as *The Secret* by Rhonda Byrne, emphasise the idea of projecting intention outward and aligning belief with desired outcomes. While the language may differ from scientific terminology, the practical overlap is clear: when a player consistently visualises success and emotionally connects with that image, they reduce internal resistance and increase commitment to the action.

Specificity and Decisiveness

The effectiveness of target selection is directly proportional to its specificity. A vague intention - *"I'll aim for the backhand side"* - produces less benefit than a precise commitment: *"I'm aiming for the T,"* or *"I'm hitting heavy crosscourt to push them wide."* A specific target creates a sharper internal representation, which the motor system can translate into more accurate and repeatable execution. The clearer the picture, the clearer the movement.

Decisiveness is equally important. A tentatively held target - *"I might go wide, unless I change my mind"* - introduces hesitation, which disrupts timing and fluidity. In contrast, a firmly held decision allows the body to move with conviction. Research in decision-making consistently shows that decisiveness itself improves performance under pressure, even when the chosen option is not perfect. In tennis terms, a committed shot is almost always more effective than a technically better shot executed with doubt.

Integration into Routine

In practice, this process can be completed in just a few seconds. The player selects a clear target, visualises the ball travelling to that spot, and allows a brief sense of completion or success to register. Then they step into the serve or return and execute. Over time, this sequence becomes automatic - a seamless link between intention, visualisation, and action.

In a match environment where pressure compresses time and amplifies uncertainty, this combination of pre-commitment and visualisation provides structure. It removes indecision, primes the body for execution, and aligns the player's focus with a single, clear outcome. Rather than reacting in the moment, the player steps into each point with a defined plan - seen, felt, and ready to be executed.

By the age of sixteen, the player's first-serve percentage had become a growing concern for nearly two full seasons. The issue was not technical. His coach remained satisfied with the mechanics of the serve itself. The motion was fluid, repeatable, and efficient during training.

In practice sessions, his first-serve percentage consistently hovered around seventy-two percent. During early tournament rounds, it usually remained close to sixty-eight percent. However as matches became more important, the percentage dropped sharply.

In higher valued matches like semi-finals and finals, sometimes it dropped to as low as fifty percent.

His coach had spent considerable time trying to identify the technical reason for this decline before concluding that there was no technical reason. The serve motion was the same. The ball toss was the same. The court speed and conditions were the same. The only variable that changed as the match became more important was the process by which the serve was selected.

In low-pressure situations, the player selected his serve target early, committed to it fully, and allowed the body to execute freely. Under pressure, however, the decision-making process became chaotic. He started to change his mind late, sometimes multiple times. He began the motion without complete commitment to the target. Occasionally, he arrived at the toss still uncertain whether he was serving wide, body, or down the T.

Internally, the process felt rushed and overcrowded. Thoughts accelerated. Anxiety created urgency. Instead of one clear instruction, the body received competing signals simultaneously. The serve itself was not breaking down, the decision preceding it was.

The solution was technical in structure but psychological in nature: he was instructed to select his serve target while bouncing the ball - during the bounce sequence - and to not begin the service motion until the selection was completely final. If the ball bounce ended and a target had not been selected, he was to bounce again until it had.

In the next tournament, his first serve percentage remained consistent across all rounds for the first time in his junior career. In the final - the highest-pressure match - it was approximately seventy-five percent.

The improvement did not come from serving harder or faster, it came from committing to his decision earlier. The body already possessed the skill. What pressure had disrupted was the clarity of instruction being sent to it. Simply resolving the decision before the execution began, giving the body the singular instruction it needed to perform the skill it already possessed.

CHAPTER 25

Watch the Ball in Hand Before Serving

> 💡 **PRACTICAL TIP:** Before you toss, spend two seconds watching the ball sitting still in your hand. This pre-serve focus act quiets the mind, centres attention, and primes your toss for consistency.

The ball in the server's hand before the serve represents the last moment of complete, uncontested control the player will have during that point. After the toss, the ball is in the air, its trajectory governed by physics and environmental variables. After contact, it enters the opponent's domain, and the point becomes reactive. These few seconds before the toss are therefore a uniquely valuable window - the final opportunity for deliberate, composed attention before performance shifts into rapid execution.

The act of watching the ball in the hand - attending to its texture, its weight, its stillness - capitalises on this window by providing a simple, controllable focal point. In doing so, it quiets the cognitive noise that often builds between points: evaluation of the previous rally, anticipation of the next, awareness of score and consequence. Rather than attempting to suppress these thoughts directly, the player redirects attention toward a neutral, immediate sensory experience.

The Ball as a Mindfulness Object

In formal mindfulness practice, attention is anchored to a simple object - often the breath or a physical sensation - to stabilise awareness in the present moment. The ball in the serving hand performs the same function in a tennis-specific context. It is always available, always stable, and inherently neutral. It carries no judgement, no outcome, no narrative. It simply exists.

When the player genuinely looks at the ball - noticing its seams, its colour contrast, the way it sits in the fingers - the visual system becomes engaged in a focused, low-demand task. This has a measurable effect on attention. The brain shifts from internally driven processing (thoughts, worries, analysis) to externally anchored perception. In practical terms, this reduces mental clutter and creates a brief but meaningful reset in awareness.

From a neurophysiological perspective, this process is supported by the way visual information is transmitted from the retina through the optic nerve to the brain's visual and attentional networks. A stable, single-point gaze - particularly on a near object - reduces the need for rapid eye movements (saccades), which are often associated with scanning and heightened alertness. Fewer saccades can correspond with a more settled attentional state. In contrast, when the eyes are darting or unfocused, the brain is typically processing a higher volume of competing stimuli, which can contribute to cognitive overload.

There is also an indirect calming effect on the autonomic nervous system. While the optic nerve itself is not responsible for regulating emotional state, the act of sustained, steady visual fixation can support a shift away from heightened sympathetic activation (fight-or-flight) toward a more regulated state. This is partly because focused attention on a simple stimulus reduces uncertainty and unpredictability - two key drivers of stress responses. The result is subtle but important: reduced muscle tension, more stable breathing, and improved coordination.

Visual Stillness and Motor Preparation

The stillness of the ball in the hand has additional implications for motor control. Before any complex movement, the nervous system benefits from a moment of stability. Watching the ball reinforces this stillness - both visually and physically. The hand becomes steady, the grip more consistent, and the body momentarily settles into alignment.

This moment of stillness acts as a reference point for the movement that follows. The serve is a highly coordinated sequence requiring precise timing and spatial accuracy. Beginning that sequence from a calm, stable starting point increases the likelihood of consistent execution. In contrast, initiating the serve from a distracted or hurried state often results in variability - particularly in the toss.

Consistency of Toss Through Pre-Serve Focus

There is also a direct technical benefit to watching the ball before serving. The toss is one of the most variable and pressure-sensitive components of the service motion. Under stress, it is often the first element to break down - drifting forward, backward, or laterally, which then forces compensations in the swing.

By attending carefully to the ball in the hand before initiating the toss, the player enhances proprioceptive awareness in the fingers, wrist, and forearm. This improves the precision of the release. The brain effectively "maps" the starting position more clearly, allowing the subsequent movement to be more controlled. In addition, the focused visual attention creates a clearer internal representation of where the ball should travel, supporting more accurate placement.

Integration into Routine

In practice, this technique is simple and brief. Before beginning the service motion, the player allows their gaze to settle on the ball for one to two seconds. During this time, attention is fully directed to the object - not passively, but deliberately. This can be paired with a breath or a physical cue, but it does not need to be complex.

Over time, this small act becomes a reliable pre-serve ritual. It marks the transition from between-point recovery to point initiation. The player moves from a potentially scattered or emotionally charged state into one of clarity, stability, and readiness. The ball is no longer just an object to be struck - it becomes the anchor that prepares the mind and body to perform.

★ REAL-LIFE EXAMPLE ★

The player had double faulted at 30-40 and lost the game from a position of dominance in more matches than he could count. Always on second serve. Always at the worst moment. The toss on second serve under pressure had become unreliable - drifting slightly behind him, causing the serve motion to compensate with excessive muscle rather than clean technique.

The coach had filmed multiple service games across four tournaments and analysed the toss in high pressure versus low pressure situations. The finding was clear: in low-pressure situations, he watched the ball in his hand for an average of 1.8 seconds before the toss. In high-pressure situations, this pre-toss observation period dropped to 0.4 seconds - barely a glance.

The intervention was simple: he was instructed to watch the ball in hand for a minimum of two seconds before every serve, regardless of the score. Not to think about anything in particular during those two seconds - just to look at the ball. Feel it. See it.

The player initially found this difficult to implement under match conditions because the two-second pause felt conspicuous and slow, almost self-conscious. But as the coach pointed out, professional servers routinely take considerably longer with their pre-serve routine than ordinary players do, and that the time was well within the legal interval.

The toss improvement was measurable within two sessions. With genuine pre-toss attention to the ball, his toss placement under pressure became nearly identical to the practice placement - the drift disappeared almost entirely. And with a consistent toss came a consistent motion and, consequently, a more reliable serve. He had time, and he used it well.

In the next tournament, he double faulted twice in the entire tournament - down from an average of four to six double faults per match. Both double faults occurred in routine situations rather than pressure situations. The pressure double fault - the one that had haunted him for two seasons - essentially disappeared.

He told his coach afterward that the strangest thing about the technique was how little he had to do. He just had to look at the ball. 'It seems too simple,' he said. 'I kept waiting for there to be a second part.'

'There is no second part,' the coach said. 'That's the whole thing.'

CHAPTER 26

Track Your Opponent Calmly Between the Points

> 💡 PRACTICAL TIP: Observe your opponent between points as a source of tactical information, not emotional comparison. Calm, objective tracking gives you an advantage without costing you composure.

Not all visual attention between points should be directed inward or at neutral objects. The opponent is a legitimate and important source of information - about their physical state, their tactical patterns, their emotional temperature, and their positioning tendencies. The challenge is learning to observe this information objectively rather than reactively. When used correctly, opponent observation becomes a strategic tool; when used poorly, it becomes a source of distraction and emotional instability.

The distinction between objective observation and reactive observation is critical. Reactive observation generates emotional responses: *"They look very confident"* (triggers anxiety), *"They're not even breathing hard"* (triggers discouragement), *"They're staring at my backhand again"* (triggers self-consciousness). Objective observation, by contrast, strips away interpretation and focuses only on what is directly measurable: *"They've stepped inside the baseline on second serve returns," "They've gone crosscourt on the last three forehands," "Their between-point routine has slowed."* One is narrative-driven; the other is data-driven.

The mind naturally tends toward interpretation because human beings are wired to assign meaning to social signals. Facial expressions, posture, movement speed, and tone of behaviour are automatically processed by the brain as indicators of threat, confidence, dominance, or vulnerability. In competitive environments, this process becomes amplified. A player may unconsciously interpret an opponent's confident walk as evidence that they are "in control" or interpret visible frustration as evidence that they are "collapsing." The problem is that these interpretations are often inaccurate and, more importantly, emotionally costly. Objective observation removes this layer of assumption and keeps attention anchored to information that is genuinely useful.

A key part of developing this skill is learning not to be influenced by the opponent's personal behaviours or on-court antics. Many players, intentionally or not, display behaviours designed to project confidence, disrupt rhythm, or create psychological pressure - exaggerated body language, extended routines, eye contact, vocal expressions, or visible frustration. These behaviours can easily pull an opponent into an emotional reaction if interpreted personally. The disciplined player, however, treats all of this as neutral information.

A useful mindset shift is to approach opponent observation as if it were a form of applied science. You are not engaging with the opponent on an emotional level; you are observing a system in motion. Their behaviours are not statements about you - they are outputs of their own internal state. By viewing the opponent through this lens, the player creates psychological distance. The question is no longer *"What does this mean about me or the match?"* but rather *"What does this tell me about their current tendencies?"*

This detachment has a stabilising effect. Emotional reactions tend to amplify physiological responses - increased heart rate, muscle tension, narrowed attention. Objective observation, on the other hand, keeps the nervous system more regulated by removing the personal significance attached to what is being seen. The player remains externally aware without becoming emotionally entangled. This allows for clearer thinking, better decision-making, and more consistent execution.

The Three Questions of Objective Opponent Tracking

A useful framework for objective between-point opponent observation is to briefly consider three simple questions: *What is their physical state? What pattern have I noticed in the last few games? What should I adjust accordingly?* These questions provide structure, directing attention toward actionable information and away from interpretation or judgement.

For example:

- *Physical state*: Are they breathing heavily? Moving slower to wide balls? Recovering more slowly between points?

- *Patterns*: Are they favouring crosscourt exchanges? Serving predominantly to one location under pressure? Avoiding a particular shot?

- *Adjustment*: Can I extend rallies? Change direction earlier? Target a specific area more consistently?

This framework does not need to be applied in depth after every point. A brief, two-second observation - one clear piece of information - is sufficient. The goal is not to analyse everything, but to build the habit of selective, purposeful awareness.

Importantly, this approach also protects the player from being drawn into psychological games. Whether the opponent is celebrating loudly, showing frustration, delaying play, or attempting to assert presence through body language, the response remains the same: observe, note, and return focus to your own process. The behaviour is neither resisted nor absorbed - it is simply *seen*.

Over time, this habit transforms the way the player experiences competition. The opponent is no longer a source of emotional fluctuation, but a source of information. Their actions become data points rather than triggers. This shift not only improves tactical clarity but also strengthens emotional control, allowing the player to compete with greater consistency and composure regardless of the behaviours presented across the net.

★ REAL-LIFE EXAMPLE ★

The semi-final match had reached a point of real intensity. Both players were within one game of each other in every set, and the quality of the tennis had produced a small crowd of spectators who had stopped to watch from outside the fence.

The player had always been a tactically aware player. His coaches consistently described him as someone who 'saw the game well' - who could identify patterns and make adjustments between games. His weakness was that under pressure, his tactical observation ability switched off entirely, replaced by reactive emotional processing. This particular match, he played an opponent who was 2 years older than him, more built and a full 30 centimetres taller in stature.

In this match, at 3-4 in the second set, he became aware that he had not consciously observed his opponent for the last four games. He had been competing intensely - playing good tennis - but operating entirely from ingrained patterns rather than live tactical adaptation. He had not noticed that his opponent had, over the last six games, significantly shortened their swing on the backhand. This was a sign of fatigue - a technique modification that also reduced the pace and depth of the backhand, creating a more attackable ball.

The player noticed it at 3-4 and began to target the backhand. The result was immediate: the shorter-swing backhand, already compromised by fatigue, became increasingly unreliable under targeting pressure. Two of the next three points ended in backhand errors from the opponent. He went on to win the second set 6-4 and then the Super Tiebreak.

After the match, his coach asked him when he had noticed the backhand change.

'What were you doing between points for the previous four games?' his coach asked.

'Surviving,' he said honestly.

His coach nodded. 'Surviving is fine. But surviving with your eyes open is better.' The training objective for the following month was clear: observe one tactical detail about the opponent between every third point, regardless of the competitive context. Not every point - just a consistent habit of tactical observation that would keep the analytical mind engaged even when the emotional mind was fully occupied with competing.

PART FIVE

MOVEMENT RESETS

Movement is medicine. The four strategies in this section use the player's movement between points as a deliberate regulation tool - changing internal state through physical action, establishing rhythm, and creating the temporal space needed to reset before the next point begins.

CHAPTER 27

Walk in a Small Circle Behind the Baseline

> 💡 **PRACTICAL TIP:** After a difficult point, walk in a small, deliberate circle behind the baseline. The movement disrupts the mental replay loop and creates space between the past point and the next one.

The circle walk is a movement reset strategy that serves the specific function of breaking cognitive fixation through a combination of physical displacement and novel movement pattern. Where the walk to the back fence provides linear displacement - moving away from the site of the error in a straight line - the circle walk adds a rotational dimension that further disrupts the cognitive loop by introducing a movement pattern that differs from ordinary court movement. This change in direction is subtle but powerful: instead of reinforcing the forward–backward rhythm of play, the player momentarily steps outside it.

Cognitive fixation - the persistent mental replaying of a specific event - is maintained, in part, by the stability of the surrounding environment. When everything around the fixating mind remains the same, the mind has nothing new to engage with, and the loop continues. Movement - and particularly movement that changes the visual and physical field - provides the novelty that interrupts this maintenance. As the player walks a small circle, their visual perspective shifts continuously: the net moves in relation to their body, the opponent briefly drops out of central view, the court geometry rotates. This dynamic change in perspective gives the brain new sensory input to process, which competes with and weakens the repetitive mental loop.

From a motor and perceptual standpoint, the circle walk also re-engages coordination in a different way to typical match play. Tennis movement is largely linear and lateral - forward, backward, side-to-side. Rotational walking introduces a different pattern of foot placement, balance adjustment, and spatial orientation. This recruits additional proprioceptive input - awareness of body position and movement - which helps draw attention back into the body. The player is no longer mentally "stuck" in the last point; they are physically engaged in a new, controlled action.

There is also a regulatory effect on the nervous system. Repetitive, rhythmic movement - particularly when it is smooth and controlled - can help stabilise internal arousal levels. The circle walk, when performed at a steady pace, introduces a gentle rhythm that contrasts with the abrupt, high-intensity bursts of play. This contrast allows the body to downshift slightly from the peak activation of the rally, without losing readiness. It is not a full relaxation; it is a recalibration.

The Symbolic Function of the Circle

Beyond its neurological interruption function, the circle walk also carries a useful symbolic meaning for the player who has incorporated it as a deliberate practice. Walking a circle is, literally and figuratively, a way of going around - of returning to the same starting point through a different path. For a tennis player, this mirrors the structure of the match itself:

each point begins and ends in the same space, but the path taken - and the outcome - is always different.

This symbolism can be harnessed intentionally. The act of completing the circle can represent the completion of the previous point - regardless of whether it was won or lost. By physically closing the loop, the player creates a clear boundary between past and present. The message is simple: that point is done; this one is new. This is particularly valuable in moments where emotional residue from the previous rally is strong. The body performs the reset, and the mind follows.

Some players find it helpful to attach a simple internal cue to this movement - not a complex thought, but a brief acknowledgment such as *"reset"* or *"next."* Others prefer to let the movement itself carry the meaning without verbal reinforcement. Either approach is effective, provided the action is intentional.

Practical Application and Discipline

The circle walk should be small and controlled - a subtle loop rather than an exaggerated movement. It is not about drawing attention or disrupting the flow of the match, but about creating a personal reset within it. It can be used selectively, particularly after emotionally charged points, errors that trigger rumination, or moments where the player feels mentally "stuck."

Like all between-point strategies, its effectiveness depends on consistency and intention. A distracted or rushed circle walk will not produce the same effect as one performed with awareness. The player should feel the steps, notice the shift in perspective, and allow the movement to complete fully before returning to position.

Over time, the circle walk becomes another tool in the player's reset system - a way to physically and mentally step out of the past and re-enter the present. In a sport defined by repetition and momentum, the ability to deliberately interrupt unhelpful patterns - both mental and physical - is a significant advantage. The circle is simple, but its effect, when used with purpose, is profound: it closes one moment and prepares the next.

His coach had noticed the pattern in the second set: whenever the player lost three consecutive points, the fourth point was almost invariably also lost. Not because of strategic problems - the tactical approach was generally appropriate, but because the third loss had initiated a cognitive loop that was still running during the fourth point.

The player was aware of the pattern himself. He had described it to his coach: 'I know I should let it go, but I can't stop thinking about the last two shots while the fourth point is happening.' He was competing on two levels simultaneously - executing the current point while his mind was still processing the previous ones - and dividing the available cognitive resources accordingly.

The circle walk had been suggested by a sports psychologist who worked with the state junior programme. The instruction was specifically targeted at the three-consecutive-point loss scenario: after the third loss in a row, before returning to position, the player walks in a small circle behind the baseline. The circle must be completed - both directions of the walk must be included - before resuming position.

The player found the technique more effective than he expected. The physical requirement of completing the circle gave him something specific to do with the urgency that typically drove him straight back into the next point. The movement of the circle seemed to work as the psychologist had described: a movement that went around the fixation rather than through it, emerging at a different angle.

In the next tournament, the three-consecutive-loss pattern - which had persisted across the entire previous season - occurred twice. In both instances, he implemented the circle walk. In both instances, he won the fourth point and then the game. The pattern had not been eliminated - no single technique eliminates deeply conditioned patterns completely - but it had been disrupted at the point of its previous greatest strength.

CHAPTER 28

Slow Down Your Walking Pace Deliberately

> 💡 **PRACTICAL TIP:** If you feel yourself rushing between points, consciously slow your walk by half. Your pace communicates your internal state - to yourself as much as to anyone watching.

The speed at which a player moves between points is one of the most reliable visible indicators of their internal state. Experienced coaches, watching a player they know well, can read the emotional temperature of a match almost entirely from movement pace. A player who is calm, focused, and in control moves with measured deliberateness. A player who is anxious, frustrated, or feeling the pressure of momentum loss moves with an urgency that their feet cannot conceal.

What is often overlooked is that movement pace is not just a reflection of internal state - it is also a mechanism for regulating it. The tempo of walking, turning, retrieving balls, and returning to position creates a behavioural rhythm that the nervous system tends to follow. When that rhythm becomes rushed and erratic, the body remains in a heightened state of readiness, even when it is no longer required. This sustained activation can subtly degrade timing, increase muscle tension, and reduce the player's ability to make clear, composed decisions.

Human beings naturally synchronise internally with the tempo of their own behaviour. Fast, abrupt movement tends to encourage faster breathing, quicker thought patterns, and heightened emotional activation, while slower and more controlled movement promotes the opposite effect. This process is often unconscious: the nervous system interprets behavioural tempo as information about the level of threat or urgency present in the environment. In this way, deliberately slowing movement between points acts as a signal of safety and control, helping stabilise both physiological and psychological state before the next rally begins.

From an exercise physiology standpoint, rapid between-point movement keeps heart rate elevated and limits the body's ability to partially recover between rallies. Tennis is an intermittent sport, and the quality of performance depends not just on peak output during points, but on how effectively the body can reset in the short intervals between them. Slower, more controlled movement allows for micro-recovery - small reductions in heart rate, more efficient breathing patterns, and a slight release of unnecessary muscular tension. Over the course of a match, these small differences accumulate, influencing both physical endurance and mental clarity.

The pacing of movement also influences coordination. When players rush, their movements often become less precise - steps are shorter or misaligned, posture becomes more upright, and transitions between actions lose fluidity. By contrast, deliberate movement reinforces coordination and balance. Each step is placed with intention, posture is maintained, and the body remains organised. This carries forward into the next point, where movement efficiency and shot preparation are directly affected by how the player has reset.

The Counterintuitive Strategy

Slowing down when the match is accelerating - when momentum is shifting, when urgency is building, when every instinct says *"faster"* - is one of the most counterintuitive yet consistently effective strategies in competitive tennis. It often feels unnatural because it runs against the body's stress-driven impulses. Under pressure, the instinct is to speed up, to act quickly, to "do something" to regain control. Slowing down can feel like hesitation or even weakness.

In reality, it is a form of control. The player who deliberately moderates their pace is not conceding anything - they are setting the terms of engagement. By establishing a consistent, unhurried rhythm between points, they create a stable platform from which to compete. This stability allows for better decision-making, clearer tactical thinking, and more reliable execution.

There is also a perceptual effect on the opponent. Movement pace is highly visible, and players instinctively read it as a signal of composure or pressure. A player who rushes appears reactive; a player who moves with calm deliberation appears composed and in control. This perception can influence the opponent's mindset, subtly shifting pressure back across the net.

Importantly, slowing down does not mean disengaging or becoming passive. The movement remains purposeful - walking with intent, preparing deliberately, arriving at position ready to play. The difference lies in the absence of urgency.

The player is no longer being driven by the pace of the previous point or the emotional momentum of the match. They are operating at a pace they have chosen.

Over time, this becomes a defining characteristic of competitive maturity. The player learns to recognise when their movement speed is being dictated by emotion rather than intention, and to adjust accordingly. In doing so, they gain a practical tool for managing pressure that requires no technical change, no additional skill - only awareness and discipline. In a sport where margins are small and momentum shifts quickly, the ability to control tempo between points becomes a quiet but decisive advantage.

★ REAL-LIFE EXAMPLE ★

The footage from the previous tournament was unambiguous. In games where the player was behind on the scoreboard, his walking pace between points was measurably faster than in games where he was ahead or level. The difference was not dramatic - perhaps ten to fifteen percent - but it was consistent across every match reviewed.

His coach showed him the footage. The player watched himself rushing between points in the third set of a close match and recognised the pattern immediately. 'I look like I'm panicking,' he said.

'You're not panicking,' his coach said. 'But your feet think you are.'

At this stage, he had been playing competitive junior tennis for six years and now stepped up to play in the Men's Money Open Tournament which brought a different kind of pressure. He had a well-developed understanding of the mental side of the game and already had a healthy toolkit of self-regulation strategies. What surprised him about the footage was not the existence of the pattern but its unconsciousness. He had not known he was doing it. His feet had been panicking before his mind even noticed.

The training intervention over the following month was specific: in all practice matches and drills that involved score-keeping, he was required to deliberately slow his walking pace at the conclusion of any point played from a losing position. Not in all circumstances - only when behind. That was the situation where the pattern appeared most clearly, so that was where the habit had to be trained.

At first, the slower walk felt unnatural and almost too deliberate. After losing a point, his instinct was to rush back to the baseline and get on with it. Slowing down felt like wasting time. But gradually, the space created by the slower walk began to do its job.

There was more time to breathe. More time for the shoulders to drop. More time to notice whether his grip had tightened or whether his thoughts had started racing ahead to the next mistake.

Within a month, something unexpected had also occurred: he began winning more games from behind. Not because his tennis had changed significantly, but because the moments between points had changed. The panic had less room to carry him straight into the next rally.

His coach reflected afterward that this was exactly the mechanism he had hoped to create: slow the feet, create space, fill the space with regulation.

The feet were not the destination; they were the door.

CHAPTER 29

Take a Pause Before Stepping to the Line

> 💡 **PRACTICAL TIP:** Before walking to the service line or the return position, pause for one or two full seconds. This brief stillness is the last regulation opportunity before the point begins - use it deliberately.

In the architecture of the between-point interval, the final action before re-engaging with the court carries particular importance. Everything that has preceded it - the turn, the walk, the fence tap, the breathing, the string adjustment, the target selection - has been preparation. The pause before stepping to the line is the moment in which all of this preparation is consolidated, and the player commits to the next point.

The pause is not merely an absence of movement. It is a deliberately held moment of stillness - a brief but intentional state of physical and mental readiness before action. In a sport characterised by almost continuous motion, moments of stillness are rare and therefore powerful when they are deliberately created. This stillness acts as a boundary: what has happened is complete; what is about to happen is about to begin.

From a nervous system perspective, deliberate stillness interrupts the tendency to carry residual momentum from the previous point into the next one. Without a pause, players often transition directly from emotional reaction into immediate preparation, bringing tension, frustration, or urgency forward with them. The brief moment of stillness creates separation. It allows breathing to settle, posture to stabilise, and attention to consolidate around the present task rather than the previous rally. In this sense, the pause functions as a final reset point - the moment where preparation becomes readiness.

The Neuroscience of Pre-Performance Stillness

Research in motor control and sports science has consistently demonstrated that a brief period of stillness immediately before performance execution improves the quality of the subsequent motor act. This is related to the concept of preparatory neural activity - the brain's establishment of the movement programme for a skilled action before the movement begins. When the player pauses before stepping to the line, they are allowing this preparatory activity to organise fully, resulting in a cleaner, more coordinated execution.

During this moment, the nervous system is effectively "setting the stage." Competing neural signals are reduced, irrelevant muscle activation is quietened, and the intended movement pattern becomes more dominant. From a physiological standpoint, this contributes to smoother timing, more efficient sequencing of muscle activation, and a reduction in the small coordination errors that often appear under pressure.

In clinical performance psychology, this practice is related to the concept of the pre-performance routine - the structured sequence of activities that creates a consistent cognitive and physiological context for performance. The pause is the final element of this routine, serving as the transition point between preparation and execution. It is where the player stops doing and starts *being ready*.

Integrating Visualisation into the Pause

Within this still moment, there is also an opportunity to briefly integrate visualisation - not as a separate, extended exercise, but as a natural continuation of the target selection process described earlier. With the body still and attention stabilised, the player can allow a short, clear image of the upcoming point to form: the intended serve placement, the anticipated return, or the first shot pattern they are committing to.

Because the pause has already reduced cognitive noise, this visualisation tends to be sharper and more effective than if attempted in a rushed or distracted state. The image does not need to be complex. A simple, precise representation - the ball travelling to the chosen target, the body moving into position, the first shot executed with intent - is sufficient. The key is clarity and conviction, not detail.

This process reinforces the neural preparation already taking place. As referenced earlier in the discussion on visualisation, mentally rehearsing the intended outcome activates the same pathways involved in execution. When paired with stillness, this activation becomes more focused and less interrupted. The result is a stronger link between intention and action.

Commitment and Transition to Action

The pause also serves as a commitment point. Up until this moment, the player has been preparing, adjusting, and selecting. Once the pause is complete, there is no further analysis - only execution. This distinction is critical. Many performance errors occur not because of poor technique, but because the player continues to think and adjust during the action itself. The pause draws a clear line: preparation ends here.

Physically, the player should feel balanced, grounded, and composed. The posture is set, the breathing is steady, and the body is neither rushed nor passive. Mentally, there is a single, clear intention - already chosen, briefly visualised, and ready to be carried out.

From this position, the step to the line becomes purposeful. It is not a continuation of between-point movement, but the beginning of the point itself. The player moves from stillness into action with clarity and control, rather than from motion into more motion.

Over time, this final pause becomes one of the most reliable elements of the player's routine. Regardless of what has happened in the match - momentum shifts, errors, pressure moments - this moment remains constant. It provides a consistent entry point into performance, where preparation is gathered, intention is confirmed, and execution begins from a place of stability.

The final had reached its deciding moment. Match point - for either player - had appeared four times in the previous nine points, and each time it had been saved by the receiving player through a combination of aggressive returning and opponent errors. The crowd had grown significantly as other tournament matches concluded and spectators migrated to watch what was clearly the match of the day.

The player was aged fifteen, was serving at 16-15 in the super-tiebreak. The previous three serves had all been faults or weak deliveries. He was aware of every element of pressure simultaneously: the match point he needed to avoid, the first-serve percentage that had deteriorated across the tiebreak, the heaviness that started creeping into his arm, the waiting opponent who was reading his service motion with increasing confidence.

The player had walked through his complete between-point routine. He had breathed. He had bounced the ball five times - one more than usual. He had selected a target - wide to the forehand, the least expected direction given the previous serves to the backhand. He had visualised the serve landing.

Then he paused.

He stood behind the baseline for two full seconds, completely still. The ball in hand. The target in mind. His feet on the ground, pressed slightly against the court surface. His shoulders low. His breathing measured. He visualised the win in his pause. For the first time in several points, nothing was rushing.

Those two seconds felt, inside them, much longer. The court was very quiet. He became aware of details - the slight warmth of the sun on his left arm, the texture of the ball against his fingertips, the solid ground beneath his feet. He was here. The next point had not happened yet. This moment was complete in itself.

He stepped to the line and served. The serve landed wide to the forehand - not perfectly, perhaps a centimetre or two shorter than ideal - but firmly in the box and to the intended location. His opponent, surprised by the direction, sent a weak return to the centre of the court. The player stepped forward and struck a forehand winner down the line.

17-15. Won by 2. He had survived the most nail-biting super tiebreak of his life! The pause had not made the serve perfect. But it had made him present for it. And presence, on the last serve that matters in a match that matters, is everything.

CHAPTER 30

Shadow Swing Slowly Once

> 💡 **PRACTICAL TIP:** After a technically poor shot, execute one slow, deliberate shadow swing before returning to position. This replaces the motor memory of the error with the correct movement pattern.

Motor learning research has established that the most recent repetition of a movement pattern has a disproportionate influence on the quality of the subsequent repetition. In neuroscience, this is often described in terms of short-term motor memory and neural priming: the nervous system is constantly updating its "best guess" of how to perform a movement based on the most recent input. For a tennis player who has just made an error, this creates a problem - the last encoded version of the stroke is flawed, and unless it is interrupted, that faulty pattern can subtly carry forward into the next execution.

Shadow swinging - executing a slow, deliberate version of the stroke without the ball immediately after an error - directly addresses this issue. By physically performing a more accurate version of the movement, the player provides the nervous system with a corrected reference point. In effect, they overwrite or dilute the previous motor trace with a cleaner one. When the stroke is required again under match conditions, the most recent "map" available to the brain is closer to the desired pattern, increasing the likelihood of improved execution.

From an exercise physiology perspective, this process is closely tied to neuromuscular coordination and motor unit recruitment. Skilled movement depends on precise timing and sequencing of muscle activation across multiple joints - what is often referred to as intermuscular coordination. When an error occurs, this sequencing is slightly disrupted. A slow, controlled shadow swing allows the player to re-establish correct activation patterns, particularly in the kinetic chain: legs initiating movement, hips rotating, trunk transferring energy, and the upper limb delivering the racquet. Because there is no time pressure or ball to react to, the nervous system can refine these sequences with greater accuracy.

Slow Motion for Motor Precision

The critical qualifier in the strategy title is *slowly*. A rushed shadow swing - performed at match speed without deliberate attention - provides little corrective value. The benefit comes from reducing movement speed to a level where the player can consciously monitor and adjust the quality of the motion. This slower pace increases the involvement of higher motor control centres in the brain, allowing for more precise calibration of the movement.

At reduced speed, proprioceptive feedback - the body's sense of position and movement - becomes more accessible. The player can feel whether weight is transferring effectively through the feet and into the shot, whether balance is maintained through contact, whether the racquet path is smooth and continuous, and whether the follow-through completes naturally. These are details that are often missed at full speed, where execution is largely automatic.

There is also a muscular benefit. Slow, controlled movement encourages appropriate muscle activation without excessive co-contraction (simultaneous tightening of opposing muscle groups), which is common under stress. This helps restore fluidity and reduces the stiffness that often accompanies errors made under pressure.

Mental rehearsal research supports this process further. Neuroimaging studies have consistently shown that imagined or lightly rehearsed movement activates many of the same neural pathways involved in full physical execution, particularly within the motor cortex, cerebellum, and supplementary motor areas. A deliberate shadow swing therefore functions not only as a physical correction, but as a neural rehearsal of the desired movement pattern. Even without ball contact, the brain is effectively practising the stroke again.

Parallels in Boxing and Other Skill-Based Sports

This approach has a clear parallel in sports such as boxing, where athletes routinely train movements in slow, controlled sequences - often referred to as shadowboxing. Boxers will deliberately slow down punches, combinations, and defensive movements to refine technique, reinforce correct mechanics, and reconnect with rhythm before returning to full-speed execution. The purpose is not to replicate fight intensity, but to reset the brain–body connection and ensure that technique remains sound.

The same principle applies in tennis. After an error, the player is not trying to simulate match speed; they are re-establishing movement quality. The slow shadow swing acts as a technical reminder - a way of saying to the body, *this is the correct pattern*. Once that pattern is re-established, speed can naturally return during play without the same level of distortion.

Comparable patterns can be observed across many precision-based sports. Golfers frequently rehearse a slow practice swing immediately after poor contact to restore tempo and sequencing before the next shot. Baseball hitters often repeat the intended swing path after a mistimed swing to recalibrate timing and bat trajectory. Basketball players similarly rehearse shooting form after a missed free throw, reinforcing correct mechanics before the next attempt. Across all of these sports, the principle remains consistent: following an error, athletes instinctively return to a cleaner version of the movement in order to stabilise both technique and confidence before re-engaging with performance speed.

This process also has a psychological benefit. Errors often create a sense of uncertainty or doubt about a particular stroke. By immediately performing a correct version of the movement, the player replaces that doubt with a physical experience of competence. This shifts the focus from *what went wrong* to *what correct execution feels like*, which is far more useful for subsequent performance.

Integration into Match Play

In practice, the shadow swing should be brief and purposeful - one or two slow, high-quality repetitions are sufficient. The emphasis is on precision, not quantity. It is most effective when performed immediately after the error, while the previous motor trace is still active.

Over time, this strategy becomes an automatic part of the player's reset routine. Instead of carrying the error forward, the player actively corrects it in real time. The body is reminded, the movement is refined, and the next opportunity to execute begins from a more stable and accurate foundation.

In a sport where small technical deviations can compound quickly under pressure, the ability to reset the motor system between points is a significant advantage. The shadow swing is simple, efficient, and grounded in well-established principles of motor learning: the last movement matters - so make it a good one.

★ REAL-LIFE EXAMPLE ★

The forehand had been his best weapon for three years.

And for the past six games, it had been his worst enemy.

Not because the technique had changed - his coach had confirmed that it had not. But because the most recent memory his body had of hitting the forehand was the previous error, and the error before that, and the one before that. By the sixth error, his forehand swing had become a hesitant, compensating motion that bore little resemblance to the fluid, confident stroke he produced in practice.

t fourteen years old, he was experiencing what his coach later described as a negative motor learning loop — each error strengthening the neural trace of the incorrect movement and making the next error slightly more likely. From the stands, the pattern had become obvious. The prescribed intervention was simple: the shadow swing.

At the next changeover, his coach gave a specific instruction. After every forehand error for the remainder of the match, the player was to perform one slow shadow swing before walking to the fence. Not quickly. Slowly. Full extension. Full follow-through. Attention placed not on the mistake, but on the feeling of the correct movement.

The instruction felt annoyingly difficult almost immediately. The instinct after an error is to escape it — to turn away, walk to the fence, reset mentally, and hope the next forehand behaves differently. Remaining in the exact location where the mistake had just occurred and rehearsing the correct motion felt unnatural and slightly uncomfortable.

But his coach had been clear: "The body learns from the most recent experience. Give it a better most recent experience."

After the next forehand error, he stopped near the baseline and performed the shadow swing slowly. He felt the racquet path extending properly across the body. He noticed the looseness in the wrist. The balance through the front leg. The finish position that had disappeared during the previous set.

Then he walked to the fence.

The fourth forehand after implementing the shadow-swing routine landed cleanly in the corner for a winner — the kind of shot that had appeared regularly during training sessions but had been absent for almost two sets. The player stood still briefly, watching where the ball had landed, before turning toward the fence.

He did not perform a shadow swing after that point.

The movement had not required correcting.

By the third set, the forehand had returned — not to perfection, but to reliability. The shadow swing had not repaired something broken. It had replaced the repeated experience of error with the repeated experience of correct movement until the correct movement once again became the body's most recent memory.

PART SIX

EMOTIONAL RELEASE (CONTROLLED)

Emotion is not the enemy of performance. Uncontrolled emotion is. The three strategies in this final section teach you to acknowledge, express, and release emotional energy in controlled ways that prevent its accumulation and allow you to compete with full intensity without being consumed by it.

CHAPTER 31

Quiet Fist Clench and Release

> 💡 PRACTICAL TIP: A small, deliberate fist clench followed by full release is a contained emotional acknowledgment that prevents feelings from building into performance-destroying reactions.

The suppression of emotion in competitive sport is a strategy that consistently fails. Research in emotion regulation shows that attempts to push feelings down - to ignore frustration, anger, or pressure - tend to increase their intensity over time. This is often referred to as a "rebound effect," where the effort required to suppress emotion actually amplifies the underlying response. From a performance perspective, this is costly. Suppression draws on attentional and working memory resources that are already under strain in competition, leaving fewer resources available for decision-making, timing, and execution.

The alternative is controlled expression: acknowledging the emotion through a brief, contained, deliberate physical action that serves as both an expression and a release. The quiet fist clench and release is designed to fulfil this function. It allows the player to recognise what they are feeling without becoming overwhelmed by it. The action is short, structured, and repeatable - fitting seamlessly into the between-point routine while preventing emotional carryover from one point to the next.

From a psychological standpoint, this approach aligns with what is known as "response modulation with awareness" - not suppressing the emotion but shaping how it is expressed. The player is not denying the emotional response; they are giving it a controlled outlet. This distinction is critical. Emotions that are acknowledged and expressed in a contained way tend to dissipate more quickly than those that are resisted or ignored.

The Mechanism of Release

The effectiveness of the fist clench as a release mechanism is grounded in the physiology of sympathetic nervous system activation. When the body perceives stress - whether from a missed opportunity, a perceived injustice, or match pressure - the sympathetic system increases muscle tone, heart rate, and readiness for action. This is useful in short bursts, but when left unmanaged, it leads to excessive tension, reduced coordination, and emotional volatility.

The fist clench works by deliberately engaging this tension in a focused and controlled manner. By tightening the hand into a firm clench, the player is effectively "matching" the body's internal state - acknowledging the activation rather than resisting it. Holding this contraction briefly increases awareness of the tension. The subsequent release - slowly opening the hand and allowing the fingers to relax - then creates a clear contrast. This contrast is important: the nervous system registers the transition from tension to relaxation more effectively when it is deliberate.

This process is closely related to principles used in progressive muscle relaxation, a well-established technique in both clinical and performance settings. By intentionally contracting and then releasing a muscle group, the brain becomes more sensitive to the difference between tension and relaxation, making it easier to down-regulate overall muscle tone. In a tennis context, this translates into reduced tightness in the forearm, shoulders, and grip - areas that directly influence stroke fluidity.

There is also a timing benefit. The structured nature of the clench-and-release sequence gives the emotional response a defined beginning and end. Instead of lingering in the background, the emotion is processed quickly and efficiently. The player experiences it, expresses it, and moves on - all within a few seconds.

The Importance of Invisibility

The "quiet" qualifier in the strategy name is significant. The fist clench should be subtle - a small, controlled contraction that does not draw attention. It is not a visible display of frustration or intensity, but a private action. This ensures that the player maintains composure externally while still addressing what is happening internally.

This matters tactically. Opponents are constantly observing body language for signs of vulnerability or instability. Overt emotional reactions - visible frustration, exaggerated gestures, or vocal expressions - provide information that can be used to apply pressure. By contrast, a contained gesture reveals nothing. The player processes their emotion without broadcasting it.

Importantly, this is not about emotional concealment for its own sake. It is about selective expression. The player is choosing when and how to express emotion in a way that supports performance rather than undermines it. The external appearance remains stable; the internal state is actively managed.

Integration with Performance

Over time, the fist clench and release become more than a reaction - it becomes a cue. The act of clenching signals recognition: *something has triggered me.* The release signals resolution: *it's done.* This simple sequence creates a clear psychological boundary between one point and the next.

It can also be paired with other elements of the between-point routine - a breath, a posture reset, or a shift in visual focus - to create a more complete reset process. The key is consistency. When used regularly, the player conditions a reliable pattern: emotion arises, it is expressed briefly and contained, and then it is released.

In high-pressure competition, where emotional swings are inevitable, the ability to regulate rather than suppress becomes a defining skill. The quiet fist clench offers a practical, physiologically grounded method for doing exactly that - transforming emotion from a disruptive force into something that is acknowledged, managed, and quickly resolved.

★ REAL-LIFE EXAMPLE ★

The player was furious!!

The call had been outrageous!! There was no other word for it.

At 30-40 on the opponent's serve - a point that would have broken the serve and given him a 5-4 lead - the ball had landed clearly inside the baseline, and his opponent had called it out. The official who was watching from outside the court had declined to overrule, stating the "my-court, my-call" rule his opponent relied upon was acceptable and allowed to stand. The player's mind started to spiral:

'... more like 'my-court my-choice if I hook the point...'

'... OUT? Or OUT of YOUR REACH?...'

'... so this is how you made it to Nationals last year you cheat!!...'

'... even Stevie Wonder could see that ball was in...'

'... unbelievable. This match is RIGGED!...'

'... wonder how much they're bribing that official...'

He felt the reaction physically before he could fully organise it mentally: heat rising sharply through the chest and neck, jaw tightening, breathing shortening. There was a sudden and overwhelming urge to say exactly what he thought about the call.

At the same time, he understood something equally important: the reaction he most wanted to express was the one he absolutely could not afford to show. Visible frustration would hand his opponent a psychological advantage and risk drawing a code violation from the official.

So he turned away from the court. His left hand (the non-racquet hand) formed into a tight fist. He held it briefly, feeling the intensity of the contraction. All of his anger concentrated into a single controlled point of tension. Then he opened the hand deliberately, spreading the fingers as wide as possible while exhaling slowly through the mouth.

The release was not magical. The anger did not disappear.

But it had been acknowledged, expressed, and contained within a physical gesture that lasted less than two seconds and was visible to nobody watching. The emotional explosion that had been building now had somewhere else to go.

He walked to the fence, completed his routine, and returned to position. The next point began.

He won it with a heavy crosscourt forehand struck with controlled aggression — the emotional energy redirected rather than suppressed. He won the following point as well. Then, on the third point, his opponent double-faulted.

Break.

He would go on to win the game, the set, and the match.

Later that evening, he wrote about the incident in his Tennis Match Journal. He noted the fury created by the bad call and the additional frustration of feeling unsupported by the official's decision. But he also recognised how quickly his mindset had begun collapsing after the point.

Most importantly, he recorded the strategy that had allowed him to regain control before the anger controlled, refocus and self-regulate.

Sometimes the situation is unfair, sometimes the call is wrong, and sometimes the most important skill in competition is the ability to regulate yourself when nothing else feels controllable. *Sometimes there's simply nothing you can do but control yourself.*

CHAPTER 32

Small Nod or 'Yes' to Yourself

> 💡 **PRACTICAL TIP:** After winning a tough point or executing something well, give yourself a single small nod or quiet 'yes.' This internal acknowledgment reinforces positive patterns and builds genuine competitive confidence.

Self-affirmation in competitive sport has a complex and sometimes misunderstood role. The popular culture of athletic motivation frequently emphasises dramatic affirmation - the raised fist, the shouted celebration, the extended emotional response to a significant point. And while these expressions have their place, the more subtle and consistently valuable form of self-affirmation is the quiet, internal acknowledgment of good execution.

The small nod or quiet "yes" - addressed to the self, barely visible or completely internal - serves as a micro-affirmation that reinforces the neural patterns associated with successful performance. From a learning science perspective, positive reinforcement of desired behaviour increases the probability of that behaviour recurring. Applied to tennis, this means that acknowledging effective execution - even at the level of a single nod - increases the likelihood of repeating that execution. It also stabilises attention, keeping the player focused on what is working rather than what has gone wrong.

Confidence as a Skill, Not a Feeling

One of the most important reframings in performance psychology is the understanding that confidence is not a feeling that arrives before performance - it is a skill that is built through accumulated acknowledgment of successful performance. Players who attribute their confidence to "feeling good" misunderstand the causal direction: confidence does not produce good performance, it is produced by recognising and reinforcing good performance.

The small nod or quiet "yes" is a practical tool for building this acknowledgment habit. It trains the player to notice, in real time, when execution meets the standard - and to mark that moment with a brief internal signal that reinforces the pattern. Over time, this reinforcement creates a genuine confidence base that is internally generated rather than externally dependent. The player is no longer waiting for confidence to appear; they are actively constructing it, point by point.

Directing Affirmation at Process, Not Just Outcome

The most valuable targets for the small nod are not necessarily point-winning shots or moments of spectacular play. They are the moments of successful process execution - the well-executed reset breath, the maintained routine under pressure, the deliberate target selection that produced the intended outcome, the forehand struck with the correct technique despite the pressure of the situation.

By affirming process as well as outcome, the player trains their attentional system to recognise and value the behaviours described throughout this book. This creates a virtuous reinforcement cycle: apply a strategy, notice its effectiveness, affirm it, and repeat. Over time, this shifts the player's focus from results to controllable actions, which is where consistent performance is built.

The Role of Controlled External Expression

While quiet affirmation should form the foundation of this habit, there are moments in competitive tennis where a more visible expression - a firmer "Yes!" or "Come on!" paired with a controlled fist pump - can be both appropriate and beneficial. Players such as Lleyton Hewitt have made this style of expression iconic, using it to generate energy, reinforce belief, and shift momentum during key moments in a match.

When used selectively and with intention, this type of external affirmation can elevate arousal to an optimal level and create a surge of competitive intensity. It can act as a psychological statement - not just to the opponent, but to oneself - that the player is engaged, committed, and ready to compete. However, the effectiveness of this expression depends on control and context.

Excessive or constant vocalisation can become counterproductive. From a physiological standpoint, repeated high-intensity emotional expression can elevate arousal beyond the optimal zone, leading to tension, rushed execution, and reduced clarity. From a behavioural and regulatory perspective, tournament environments - particularly at junior and officiated levels - often have guidelines around excessive noise or behaviour that may be considered a hindrance or unsportsmanlike conduct. Loud, prolonged, or exaggerated reactions can draw warnings from umpires and shift focus away from performance.

For this reason, the disciplined player treats external affirmation as a tool, not a default. It is used sparingly, in moments where a controlled increase in intensity is beneficial, and always within the boundaries of sportsmanship and respect for the competitive environment.

The baseline remains the quiet, internal affirmation - consistent, reliable, and free from external consequence.

Integration into Competitive Behaviour

The combination of internal and occasional external affirmation gives the player a flexible system. Most points are reinforced quietly, building steady confidence and focus. Key moments may be marked with a slightly more visible expression, used deliberately to elevate energy or reinforce momentum.

The critical factor is that the expression remains intentional rather than impulsive. Effective competitors do not allow emotional reactions to dictate their behaviour; they choose when and how to express energy. A quiet nod after disciplined execution, a controlled fist pump after a courageous point, or a brief verbal cue after sustained effort can all serve as forms of reinforcement when used purposefully. The behaviour is not performed for theatrics or external approval, but to strengthen the internal association between composure, commitment, and successful competitive action.

Over time, this approach creates emotional balance. The player is neither flat nor overly reactive. They are engaged, responsive, and in control of how they express and reinforce their performance. In a sport where emotional swings can quickly destabilise execution, the ability to affirm effectively - both internally and, when appropriate, externally - becomes a subtle but powerful component of competitive success.

The player had been taught the nod by his first tennis coach when he was still playing coloured ball. It had been introduced as a way of acknowledging effort rather than outcome - 'a way of saying thank you to the part of you that tried,' his coach had explained.

Many years later, when the player was competing at a national level, the nod had evolved into something considerably more sophisticated in its application. He used it after specific kinds of moments: a serve that landed exactly where planned under break point pressure, a tiebreak point won through an approach he had pre-selected and committed to, a reset breath that had genuinely steadied him in a moment of mounting panic.

He did not use it after every won point - that would have diluted its meaning. He used it after the points and moments that reflected the qualities he most wanted to reinforce in himself. Composure. Deliberateness. Execution under pressure. The nod had become, over years of consistent use, a calibrated signal - a way of telling himself, privately and specifically, 'that is who you are when you are at your best.'

In the championships semi-final, playing the second seed in the sixteen-and-under draw, he was broken in the fourth game of the third set. The previous three games had been close, each going to deuce, and the one that had finally gone against him had been decided by a call he disagreed with but accepted. He was angry. He was tired. He was a break down in the deciding set.

He walked to the fence and performed his routine. At the end of the routine - after the breathing, the shoulder drop, the string adjustment - he did something he had not planned: he gave himself a small nod. Not for anything specific. For still being here. For not having conceded the match in his own mind.

He broke back two games later. He won the set 7-5. After the match-winning point, the nod he gave himself was, for once, visible - his coach saw it from across the fence and recognised it immediately. Not as a celebration. As an acknowledgment. He was telling himself something only he fully understood: that the nod at the fence, at the lowest point of the set, had been where the match had truly turned.

CHAPTER 33

The Integrated Reset Routine: Building Your Personal System

> 💡 **PRACTICAL TIP:** No single strategy will save a match on its own - but a personalised, practised, and automatic between-point routine built from these strategies will transform your ability to compete under pressure.

Why Integration Matters

This book contains thirty-three distinct strategies for self-regulation in competitive tennis. Reading them, a player might be tempted to attempt all of them simultaneously - or alternatively, to feel overwhelmed by the volume of options and select none at all. Neither response serves the goal of the book.

The purpose of the variety of strategies presented here is not to create a thirty-three-step between-point protocol. It is to provide a comprehensive toolkit from which each player - at each stage of their development, with their specific temperament, strengths, and challenges - can construct a personal between-point routine that is genuinely their own.

The most effective routines are built from a small number of strategies selected for their personal relevance and practised until they are completely automatic. Four or five strategies, deeply embedded through consistent practice, produce better results than twelve strategies superficially attempted. The integration principle is: choose deliberately, practise exhaustively, deploy automatically.

Building Your Personal Between-Point Routine

The construction of a personal between-point routine should be guided by three questions. First: Which of my specific challenges does each strategy address? Different players struggle with different aspects of the competitive mental game. A player who struggles primarily with physical tension should prioritise strategies from Parts One and Three. A player who struggles primarily with cognitive fixation should prioritise strategies from Parts Two and Five. A player who struggles primarily with emotional regulation should prioritise strategies from Part Six.

Second: Which strategies feel most natural and least effortful to implement? A strategy that requires significant conscious effort to remember and apply will not be consistently available under the highest-pressure conditions. The strategies you select for your personal routine should feel relatively accessible even when you are physiologically and cognitively stressed.

Third: Which combination of strategies addresses the whole system? The most effective routines address multiple dimensions of the reset process simultaneously - physical regulation (breathing, body), attentional reset (visual focus, micro-tasks), and preparation for execution (target selection, pre-serve focus). A routine that addresses only one dimension leaves the others unmanaged.

The Four-Phase Framework

A practical framework for organising your personal routine is to think in four phases, each lasting approximately four to six seconds, giving a total routine length of sixteen to twenty-five seconds - well within the legal between-point interval.

Phase One: Disengage. The moment the point ends, turn away and take one deliberate exhale. This is the interruption phase - breaking the link between the previous point and the current moment.

Phase Two: Reset. Walk to the fence, tap it, use the towel, adjust strings, or perform whichever grounding or between-point ritual strategies you have selected. This is the regulation phase - actively managing physical and attentional state.

Phase Three: Prepare. Select your target, perform your ball bounce sequence, and watch the ball in your hand. This is the preparation phase - building the cognitive and physical readiness for the next point.

Phase Four: Commit. Pause. Take a final breath. Step to the line. Begin. This is the execution phase - the transition from preparation to performance.

The strength of this framework lies not only in the individual strategies themselves, but in the predictability of the sequence. Under pressure, the brain functions more effectively when actions are organised into clear and repeatable structures. A consistent four-phase routine reduces uncertainty, lowers decision-making demands, and provides the nervous system with a familiar pathway to follow between points. Over time, the sequence itself becomes regulating. The player no longer needs to consciously think through each step in detail; the routine begins carrying them forward automatically from disengagement to readiness.

The Commitment to Practice

The fundamental requirement for an integrated between-point routine is practice - not of the individual strategies in isolation, but of the full routine sequence in match-condition training environments. This means implementing the routine consistently in every practice point, not just matches, until the sequence is so deeply embedded that it runs automatically even when cognitive and emotional resources are fully occupied with the demands of competition.

Players who implement their between-point routine inconsistently - using it when they remember, abandoning it when they feel rushed - will not derive the full benefit of the approach. The routine's value comes precisely from its consistency: the fact that it runs regardless of the score, regardless of the emotional state, regardless of the quality of the previous point. Consistency is what transforms a collection of strategies into a system.

Build your routine. Practise it relentlessly. Trust it completely. And go play the match of your life.

★ REAL-LIFE EXAMPLE ★

Two highly ranked top tier Under 14 players met again in the tournament final. They had competed against each other twice in the previous year - with a record of one match each. Both coaches had specifically prepared their players for this opponent. Both players arrived at the final knowing exactly what they were facing. They were both hungry for the win, knowing the win would give them a spot in the national tournament next month. Additionally, they had both noticed the Wilson brand scout walking the tournament looking for potential players to sponsor. The pressure was huge.

In the warm-up, an observer watching both players would have noticed an immediate difference. One player - the number-one seed - warmed up with high energy and a kind of visible intensity that was compelling to watch. The other player - the number-two seed, the one who had been preparing methodically for this specific match - warmed up with a quality of deliberateness that was less spectacular but somehow more settled.

The first set went to the number-one seed 6-4. Not comfortably - there were six games that went to deuce, and three that went to over five deuces. The number-one seed played freely and aggressively. The number-two seed competed on every point but looked slightly cautious in the first set, as though still calibrating the match.

The changeover after the first set was the difference. The number-two seed took a brief changeover break to reset his composure and ran through a mental checklist that had been practised hundreds of times. Not about tactics - the tactical plan was already established and had not materially failed. About routine. Was the between-point sequence running consistently? Was the breathing deliberate? Was the target selection happening before the execution rather than during it?

The answers were mixed, and the player knew it. The routine had been inconsistent. The breathing had been adequate but not deliberate. Target selection had been occurring mid-preparation rather than during the ball bounce.

For the second set, the commitment was simple: routine first, tennis second. Every point, every interval, the sequence runs. Turn, walk, tap, breathe, select, pause, serve.

The second set went to the number-two seed 6-3. The match had not changed tactically. But the quality of between-point regulation had changed completely - the number-two seed was now present at the beginning of every point in a way they had not been in the first set. Present in body, in attention, and in intention.

The third set reached 5-5, then 6-6, then tiebreak. In the tiebreak, at match point, the number-two seed stood behind the baseline and ran through the routine one more time. Turn. Exhale. Fence. Tap. Breathe. Select. Ball in hand. Pause. Commit.

The serve landed in. The rally lasted eleven shots. The number-two seed won it on the eleventh - a forehand winner struck down the line from a position most players would have defended. He had to stick to his strategy and his routine. He had to trust in the process.

After the presentation ceremony, the losing coach - a highly experienced and respected figure in the junior programme - approached the winning coach and asked, genuinely curious, what had changed between sets one and three.

The winning coach thought for a moment. 'Nothing changed about how they play tennis,' he said. 'Everything changed about how they live between the points.'

PART SEVEN

With a toolbox of options available to you, the best path forward is to trial these strategies with your deepened understanding of them. Find what you like and which ones work best for you, remembering you can adapt others during competitive play.

This chapter consolidates the essential strategies from this book into a practical quick-reference format. Use this section before matches as a reminder of your toolkit, during changeovers as a mental checklist, and after matches as a reflection guide. These are not rigid rules - they are flexible tools. Select the ones that resonate most strongly with your game and build them into your personal between-point system.

🫁 BREATHING TECHNIQUES

The breath is your fastest available regulation tool. Inhale deeply through the nose before serving or returning, and exhale slowly to lower your heart rate and release accumulated tension. A particularly powerful technique: exhale for the entire duration the ball is in the air - from the moment it leaves your racquet until it bounces on your opponent's side. This extended exhale has a direct calming effect on the nervous system and prevents the breath-holding that commonly occurs under pressure. Practice the 3-count rhythm: inhale for 3 seconds before the point begins, exhale for 3 seconds as the ball travels. With experience, this becomes a fluid, automatic part of every rally - breathing with the game rather than against it.

⏱ BETWEEN-POINT ROUTINES

Establish a consistent ritual that you repeat between every single point, regardless of the outcome. This might include adjusting your strings, wiping your face with the towel, bouncing the ball a fixed number of times, tapping the fence, or spinning the racquet. The specific actions matter less than their consistency. A reliable routine reduces decision-making load, creates a psychological boundary between each point, and signals to your nervous system that a reset phase has begun. Your routine should be practised in training until it runs automatically - it is not something you remember to do when things go wrong, it is something you do every time.

🏃 PHYSICAL RELAXATION

Relax your muscles immediately after hitting the ball. Many players unconsciously hold tension in the striking arm, hand, and shoulder after contact - a pattern that accumulates across a match and significantly impairs execution quality. Keep your movements fluid rather than stiff. Between points, shake out the arms, drop the shoulders, and open the hand from the grip. The body that arrives at the next point should feel as close to fresh as possible. Physical tightness is the enemy of timing, spin, and feel - and much of it can be released with deliberate, habitual relaxation between shots and between points.

⌖ MENTAL FOCUS

Focus on the present point only. Not the last one, not the score, not what might happen if you lose this game. The present point. If you feel overwhelmed, the most effective corrective action is to deliberately slow your pace of play. Walk more slowly. Bounce the ball more times. Take an extra breath. The internal experience of slowing down physically is a direct reset for the mental acceleration that pressure produces. Use a cue word - 'here', 'now', 'ball', 'breathe' - to anchor your attention when it begins to drift toward outcomes, opponents, or spectators.

○ POSITIVE SELF-TALK

Replace negative, catastrophic thoughts with constructive, grounded alternatives. This does not mean pretending everything is fine when it is not. It means choosing thoughts that are useful rather than thoughts that are destructive. 'I've got this' is more useful than 'I always lose from here.' 'One point at a time' is more useful than 'I'm going to lose the set.' 'My forehand works - trust it' is more useful than 'My forehand is broken.' You are the commentator in your own head. Choose commentary that helps you compete rather than commentary that confirms your worst fears.

♛ MAINTAIN BALANCE - HOLD YOUR FINISH

After striking the ball, hold your finishing position until the ball bounces on the other side of the net. This single habit - which takes no additional time and requires no special equipment - has profound effects on both technical execution and psychological composure. Holding the finish encourages complete follow-through, which produces better shot quality. It forces a moment of stillness after the strike, interrupting the reactive urgency that drives rushed play. It trains balance and body control. And it creates a visual and internal signal that the shot has been executed with intent, not panic. When you hold your finish, you are declaring, in physical terms: that shot was deliberate. That is the posture of a competitor.

These six principles - breathing, routine, relaxation, focus, self-talk, and balance - form the philosophical foundation of this book. Every chapter you have read is, at some level, an elaboration of one or more of these core ideas. When you are on court and cannot remember the specific details of any chapter, return to these principles. They will guide you home.

CHAPTER 34

Visualisation: Seeing the Match Before You Play It

> 💡 **PRACTICAL TIP:** Spend five minutes before every match mentally playing through the key points - your serve pattern, your game plan, and your response to adversity. What you rehearse in the mind, the body will be more ready to execute.

What Visualisation Is - and What It Is Not

Visualisation - also called mental imagery, mental rehearsal, or guided imagery - is the deliberate construction and experience of a vivid mental simulation of a sporting performance. It is not daydreaming. It is not wishful thinking. And it is not simply imagining winning and expecting that to produce results.

Effective visualisation in sport involves specific, multi-sensory mental rehearsal of realistic, relevant competitive scenarios. The player sees the court from their own perspective, feels the racquet in their hand, hears the sound of the ball on the strings, and experiences the physical sensations of movement - all in the imagination, with the same clarity and intentionality they would bring to a practice drill.

The neurological basis for this practice is well-established. Functional MRI studies have demonstrated that when a skilled athlete vividly imagines performing a movement, the motor cortex activates in patterns that closely mirror those observed during actual physical execution. In other words, the brain cannot fully distinguish between a highly detailed imagined experience and a real one. This means that mental rehearsal produces genuine neural practice - it strengthens the same pathways that physical practice strengthens.

For tennis players, this has concrete and measurable implications. Consistent visualisation practice improves the automaticity of serve routines, the fluency of between-point habits, the confidence with which tactical decisions are made, and the quality of emotional regulation under pressure. These improvements occur in the mind, but they show up on the court.

Pre-Match Visualisation: Seeing the Game Plan

The most valuable time to practise visualisation is in the period immediately before a match - ideally in the fifteen to thirty minutes before warm-up begins, when you are physically relaxed but mentally preparing. This is the window in which a clear, calm mental run-through of the upcoming match can establish the psychological architecture for what follows.

Begin by finding a quiet space where you will not be interrupted. Sit or lie comfortably, close your eyes, and take three slow, deliberate breaths to settle your nervous system. Then begin to construct the match environment in your imagination.

See the court. Not a generic court - the specific court you are about to play on. The colour of the surface, the height of the fences, the position of the sun at this time of day, the sound of the surrounding tournament environment. Build the scene with as much detail as your imagination allows. The more specific and sensory-rich the visualisation, the more effective it will be.

Now see yourself walking onto the court. Notice how you walk - deliberately, confidently, with the measured pace described in Chapter 28. See yourself conducting your warm-up with composure. Feel the racquet in your hand during the first few warm-up groundstrokes. Notice the rhythm of your footwork. This is not a highlights reel - it is a mental practice session, and it should feel like one.

Visualising Your Game Plan - Plan A

With the scene established, move into the match itself. Visualise the tactical plan you have prepared for this specific opponent. If your game plan is to serve wide to the backhand and attack the short ball to the forehand, see that sequence unfolding clearly: the ball toss, the wide serve kicking to the backhand, the weak return landing mid-court, your approach, the forehand winner.

Run this sequence multiple times. Not because you are making promises to yourself about the outcome - you are not - but because repetition in the mental practice builds the neural readiness for that pattern to emerge fluently when the moment arrives in the match. You are pre-loading the motor programme, making it more accessible under the cognitive load of competition.

Visualise your return game plan with equal specificity. Where will you stand? How will you respond to a wide serve to your backhand? What is your first ball - a safe crosscourt, an aggressive inside-out forehand, a chip and charge? See each of these scenarios clearly. Feel the movement, the contact, the execution.

Visualising Your Game Plan - Plan B

One of the most overlooked elements of pre-match visualisation is the mental rehearsal of adversity. Most players, when they visualise, focus exclusively on their best-case scenarios - the serve going in, the forehand landing clean, the match unfolding as planned. This is understandable but incomplete.

A complete pre-match visualisation includes the scenarios where things do not go according to plan, and specifically rehearses the response to those scenarios. What will you do if you lose the first five games? See yourself at 0-5, maintaining composure, walking to the fence, performing your routine, returning to the baseline with the same measured pace. What will you do if your opponent makes a bad line call on a critical point? See yourself managing the frustration - the fist clench and release, the fence tap, the extended exhale - and competing with full intensity on the next point.

This is Plan B visualisation, and it is arguably more important than Plan A. Because Plan A often works without much mental preparation - when everything is going well, performance emerges naturally. It is when Plan B is required that mental preparation becomes the decisive factor.

Rehearse your responses to a double fault at break point. Rehearse your response to losing three consecutive games from a set up. Rehearse your response to playing in conditions you find difficult - heavy wind, intense heat, a slow clay court. See yourself applying the strategies from this book in each of these scenarios, not perfectly, but effectively. Not without emotion, but with managed emotion.

In-Match Visualisation: The Point Preview

Visualisation is not only a pre-match practice. It can and should be used within the match itself - specifically, in the seconds immediately before each point begins.

The point preview is a brief, two to three second mental flash of the intended execution that follows target selection. After selecting the serve target or return pattern during the between-point routine, the player briefly sees it happening in their mind - the trajectory of the ball, its landing in the intended location, the beginning of the rally from an advantageous position.

This is not a lengthy, detailed visualisation - there is not time for that between points. It is a quick, vivid flash of intention that connects the tactical decision to the physical execution. Research on pre-performance imagery in sport consistently demonstrates that even brief imagery in the seconds before execution improves both accuracy and confidence.

The point preview becomes particularly valuable under pressure - in tiebreaks, at break points, at match point. These are the moments when the mind is most likely to intrude on the body's ability to execute automatically. A brief, clear mental image of the intended execution displaces the intrusive thoughts that would otherwise occupy this space.

Recovery Visualisation: Getting Back on Track

Perhaps the most practically important application of visualisation for junior and developing players is the use of recovery imagery - mental rehearsal of the process of regaining composure and performance after a difficult period in a match.

This practice is done between points, during changeovers, or even at the back fence after a particularly difficult point. The player briefly visualises themselves performing the reset strategies from this book: the turn, the walk, the fence tap, the extended exhale, the shoulder drop, the string adjustment. They see themselves arriving back at the baseline in a regulated state, selecting a target with confidence, and executing with the same quality they produce in practice.

Recovery visualisation does not deny the difficulty of what just happened. It does not pretend that the frustration does not exist. It simply provides the brain with a clear, positive image of what comes next - a direction to move toward rather than a difficulty to remain stuck in.

Many players who struggle to implement the strategies in this book during matches report that the missing ingredient is not knowledge of the strategy but access to it under pressure. They know what they should do; they simply cannot find it when they need it. Recovery visualisation addresses this access problem by rehearsing the sequence so thoroughly - in the mind, in training, and in practice matches - that it becomes the default response to difficulty rather than a conscious, effortful choice.

Building a Visualisation Practice

Like all the skills in this book, visualisation improves with practice. Begin with five minutes of pre-match visualisation before every training session, not just competitive matches. The training environment provides the ideal opportunity to rehearse mental imagery skills at low stakes before deploying them in competition.

A useful structure for your pre-match visualisation session is as follows: three breaths to settle, thirty seconds of court scene construction, two minutes of Plan A game plan rehearsal including at least three specific tactical sequences, two minutes of Plan B adversity rehearsal including at least two specific difficult scenarios and your regulated responses to them, and a final thirty-second review of your between-point routine, seeing it running smoothly and automatically throughout the match.

This five-minute practice, repeated consistently over weeks and months, builds a mental match-readiness that no amount of physical practice alone can fully replicate. You have already practised the shots. Now practise the match. See it in the mind, and the body will be far better prepared to deliver it on the court.

CHAPTER 35

'Next Play Mentality'

In competitive tennis, the interval between points is not just a recovery period - it is a decision point. The player must choose, consciously or unconsciously, whether to carry the past forward or to release it and engage fully with what comes next. The "next play" mentality is the disciplined choice to disengage from the previous point - whether successful or unsuccessful - and direct full attention toward the immediate task ahead.

The concept, widely associated with the coaching philosophy of Mike Krzyzewski, reflects a simple but powerful principle: no single moment should define the next one. In practice, this means developing the ability to acknowledge what has just occurred, extract any relevant information, and then move on without emotional residue. The previous point is complete. The next point is independent.

The Cost of Looking Back

Tennis is uniquely unforgiving of mental carryover. Unlike continuous sports, where momentum can sometimes mask lapses in attention, tennis presents a clear reset opportunity before every point. When a player continues to replay a missed opportunity, argue internally with a decision, or dwell on a previous error, they are effectively competing in two timelines at once - the present point and the past one. This division of attention reduces clarity, slows reaction time, and increases the likelihood of further errors.

From a cognitive perspective, this is a problem of attentional bandwidth. The brain has limited capacity for processing information in real time. When part of that capacity is occupied by past events, less is available for reading the opponent, executing technique, and making decisions. The result is not just emotional frustration, but measurable performance decline.

The same problem occurs when attention moves too far forward into imagined future outcomes. Players begin thinking about closing out the set, protecting a lead, or avoiding a potential loss before the current point has even begun. This future-oriented thinking creates anticipatory tension and divides attention in much the same way as dwelling on the past. The next play mentality protects against both directions of distraction by continually returning focus to the only moment where performance can actually occur: the present point.

The Discipline of a Short Memory

The next play mentality is often described as having a "short memory," but this does not mean ignoring or denying what has happened. It means processing it efficiently. A missed forehand, a poor decision, or a lost point is acknowledged - not analysed repeatedly. The player recognises it, resets, and moves forward.

This is a skill, not a personality trait. Some players appear naturally able to move on quickly, but in reality, this ability is developed through deliberate practice. It is reinforced through routines, physical cues, and consistent behavioural patterns that signal closure after each point.

The key distinction is between *learning* and *lingering*. Learning occurs briefly and constructively: *What can I adjust?* Lingering is repetitive and unproductive: *Why did that happen?* The next play mentality prioritises the former and eliminates the latter.

Emotional Regulation in Real Time

Errors and setbacks in tennis are inevitable. What differentiates high-level performers is not the absence of mistakes, but the speed and effectiveness of their recovery. The next play mentality provides a framework for this recovery by emphasising emotional regulation.

When frustration arises, the player does not attempt to suppress it completely, nor do they allow it to escalate unchecked. Instead, they acknowledge it briefly and then transition forward using the reset strategies outlined in previous chapters - breath control, posture adjustment, physical movement, or a simple cue word. The emotion is experienced, processed, and released within a controlled timeframe. This prevents emotional accumulation. Without a reset, small frustrations compound, gradually increasing tension and reducing performance quality. With a consistent next play approach, each point is treated as a fresh start, limiting the carryover effect.

Intermediate Focus: One Point at a Time

At its core, the next play mentality is about narrowing focus to the smallest meaningful unit of competition: the next point. Not the game, not the set, not the match - the next action.

This aligns closely with high-performance behaviours observed across multiple sports. Elite athletes consistently demonstrate the ability to re-engage fully with the next moment, regardless of what has just occurred. In basketball, players continue to take decisive shots after misses. In football (soccer), defenders reset immediately after conceding. In tennis, the same principle applies: the next serve, the next return, the next rally.

The player's task is not to correct everything at once, but to execute the next action with clarity and intent. This simplification reduces cognitive load and increases the likelihood of effective performance.

This principle is especially visible in sports that involve repeated isolated actions under pressure. Quarterbacks in American football must reset immediately after interceptions to execute the next play effectively. Baseball hitters must approach each pitch independently regardless of previous at-bats. Golfers must fully re-engage after poor shots because emotional carryover into the next swing often produces compounding errors. Across all of these sports, elite performers distinguish themselves not by avoiding mistakes, but by limiting the amount of psychological space those mistakes are allowed to occupy afterward.

Reset Triggers: Creating the Shift

The transition from past to present does not happen automatically - it requires a trigger. This trigger can be physical, visual, or verbal, but its function is the same: to signal the end of one point and the beginning of the next. Examples include:

- Turning the back on the court immediately after the point ends
- A controlled breath or exhale
- Adjusting strings or tapping the fence
- A simple cue word such as "next" or "reset"

These triggers create a consistent pattern. The body performs the action, and the mind follows. Over time, the association becomes automatic: trigger → reset → refocus.

Confidence Through Forward Focus

One of the less obvious benefits of the next play mentality is its impact on confidence. Confidence is undermined when players dwell on mistakes, because attention is repeatedly directed toward evidence of failure. By contrast, a forward-focused mindset prevents this accumulation. Each point is treated independently, and confidence is built through present execution rather than past evaluation.

This does not eliminate pressure, but it makes it manageable. The player is no longer carrying the weight of previous errors into each new point. Instead, they approach each moment with a clean mental slate.

Application Beyond Tennis

While this chapter is grounded in tennis performance, the next play mentality is widely applicable across high-performance environments. It is used by athletes in multiple sports, by coaches managing teams under pressure, and by individuals in professional and personal contexts who must respond to setbacks quickly and effectively. The underlying principle remains the same: acknowledge, reset, move forward.

Integration into the Between-Point Routine

The next play mentality is not a standalone concept - it is the thread that connects all between-point strategies. Every action described throughout this book serves, in part, to support this transition. The physical resets, the visual anchors, the breathing patterns, and the mental cues all contribute to the same outcome: the ability to arrive at the next point fully present and ready to compete.

In practice, the sequence becomes simple:

The point ends

The reset is initiated

The past is released

The next point begins

No hesitation. No carryover. Just the next play.

Over time, this approach becomes automatic. The player no longer needs to remind themselves to move on - it becomes their default response. In a sport defined by repetition and momentum shifts, this ability is not just beneficial - it is essential.

CHAPTER 36

The Tennis Match Journal:
Planning, Recording & Reflecting

> 💡 **PRACTICAL TIP:** Write it down - before the match, during changeovers, and after the final point. A tennis match journal is not a diary; it is a performance tool that compounds your learning across every match you play.

Why a Journal Changes Everything

Every match you play contains information. Information about your own performance patterns, your emotional responses under pressure, your technical tendencies in specific situations, and the tactical tendencies of specific opponents. Without a systematic method for capturing and reviewing this information, most of it disappears within twenty-four hours - absorbed back into the general background of competitive experience without ever being processed into genuine insight.

A tennis match journal is the tool that prevents this loss. It creates a written record of your competitive experience that can be reviewed, analysed, and built upon over weeks, months, and years of competition. Players who journal consistently - who record not just scores but strategies, emotional states, cue words, and lessons - develop a self-knowledge that is simply not available to players who rely entirely on memory and intuition.

Writing itself is part of what makes journalling effective. Putting experience into words helps organise thoughts, identify patterns, and separate emotion from observation. Thoughts that feel overwhelming after a match often become clearer once written down. Journalling is therefore not just a way of recording experience, but of processing it.

This is not a new idea. Elite athletes across virtually every discipline - from professional tennis players to Olympic sprinters to elite chess players - maintain detailed records of their competitive performance. The practice is not bureaucratic or laborious when it is well-designed. It is efficient, targeted, and enormously valuable.

This chapter will guide you through the key elements of an effective tennis match journal, including how to use it before the match, during changeovers, and after the final point.

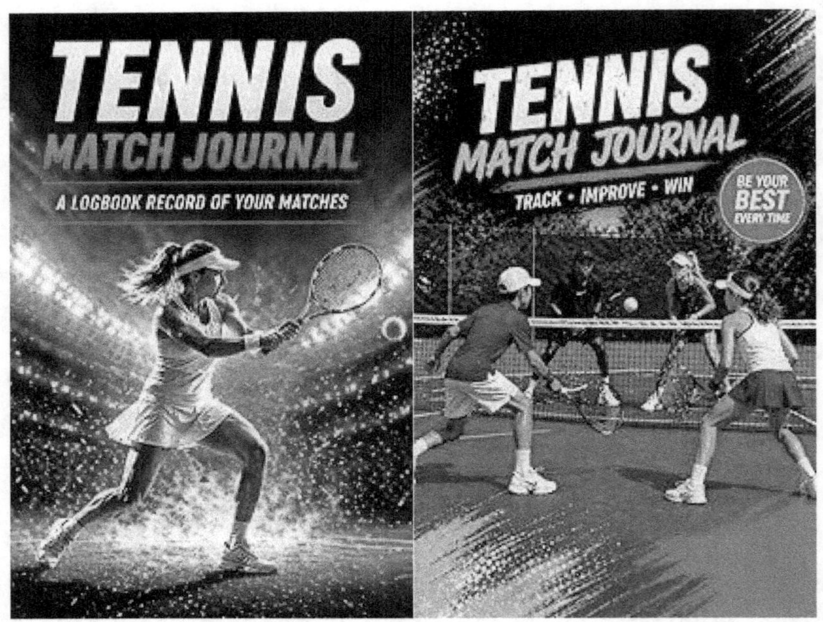

Part One: Pre-Match Planning

The most important use of your match journal happens before the match begins. A structured pre-match entry creates the cognitive architecture for everything that follows - your tactical plan, your emotional preparation, your cue words, and your contingency planning.

The Opponent Profile

If you have played this opponent before, review your previous journal entries before writing new ones. What did you notice last time? What tactics worked and which did not? Where did they attack your game most effectively? Where were their weaknesses? This review takes less than three minutes but provides genuinely useful tactical intelligence that would otherwise require the first set of the match to re-establish.

If you have not played this opponent before, record whatever you know from observation - their grip style, their preferred patterns from the deuce and advantage courts, their serve tendencies, their body language under pressure. Even small observations can become tactically significant when you are inside the match.

Court and Condition Notes

Different courts play differently. A fast hard court requires different tactical adjustments than a slow clay court. A court exposed to the prevailing wind requires different serve placement decisions than a sheltered indoor surface. Recording court-specific notes - particularly if you have played on this court or in these conditions before - provides a practical resource that you can consult and build upon across multiple visits to the same venue.

Condition notes include wind direction and intensity, temperature and sun direction, court speed assessment, and the position of the sun during warm-up (which affects ball toss and serve direction decisions). These are the environmental variables that junior players most commonly fail to account for and that experienced players systematically address.

Plan A: Your Primary Game Plan

Write your primary tactical plan for this match in two to three specific sentences. Not 'play well and stay focused' - that is not a plan. A plan is: 'Serve wide to the backhand from the deuce court, follow the wide serve with an approach to the middle, and look for the short ball to attack with the forehand.' Or: 'Return crosscourt on the backhand side to neutralise the big forehand and work the point to create a forehand opportunity from the middle of the court.'

Specificity is what makes a plan usable. A vague intention is not something you can access on a second serve at break point. A specific tactical pattern is.

Plan B: Your Contingency Plan

Plan B is your response to the scenario where Plan A is not working or where external circumstances require adaptation. Common Plan B scenarios include: your opponent returning your wide serve more effectively than expected, requiring a serve pattern change; the conditions (wind, sun) making your Plan A patterns unreliable; losing the first set and needing to change the tempo or tactical approach.

Write Plan B before the match, not during it. In the middle of a match under pressure, tactical creativity is compromised. Having a pre-written Plan B allows you to switch to it decisively rather than improvising under cognitive load.

Cue Words and Self-Regulation Actions

Record the specific cue words and physical actions you intend to use for self-regulation during this match. These should be drawn from the strategies in this book and personalised to reflect what you have found most effective in training and recent matches.

Examples: 'Exhale - fence - strings' as your between-point sequence. 'Breathe out, toes, bounce' as your pre-serve checklist. 'Walk slow - this is mine' as your self-talk cue when under pressure. Your cue words should be short, specific, and personally meaningful - words that have been tested in training and that your nervous system has learned to respond to.

Part Two: During the Match - Review

Most players treat changeovers as purely physical recovery intervals. This is understandable - they are physically demanding moments in a match. But the changeover is also the only opportunity within the match for structured reflection and planning. A brief, focused set of changeover notes can redirect the second set with information that the first set has generated.

A changeover journal review can be a useful tool and need take no more than thirty seconds. It might remind you what pattern has been most effective, what your opponent is doing differently from what you expected, whether you need to adjust your self-regulation routine, and one specific tactical intention for the next two games.

Part Three: Post-Match Reflection

The post-match journal entry should be completed within thirty minutes of the final point - while the experience is still fresh and before the emotional distance that time creates has obscured the most valuable details. It is best completed before speaking extensively to coaches, parents, or other players about the match, as external perspectives can shape your own recollection before you have recorded it independently.

What Worked

Record specifically what went well - not 'I played OK' but 'my wide serve on the deuce court was effective in the second set,' or 'my between-point routine stayed consistent even when I was down 1-4.' Positive specificity is what enables you to reliably repeat your successes. If you cannot articulate specifically what worked, you cannot systematically reproduce it.

What to Improve

Record one or two specific areas for improvement - not criticisms, but observations. 'My return of serve from the advantage court was reactive rather than planned - I need to select a return direction before the serve.' Or: 'My shoulder tension built up through the third set and I did not address it until it had already affected my serve.' These observations become the agenda for the next training session.

What You Learned

Record one specific lesson from the match that you want to carry forward. This might be about your own game, about a specific opponent, about a particular court or condition, or about a self-regulation strategy that proved more or less effective than expected. This is the entry that compounds most powerfully over time - a library of personal competitive learnings that belongs entirely to you.

The Cumulative Power of the Match Journal

The full value of a tennis match journal does not become apparent after one entry, or five, or even ten. It becomes apparent after fifty entries - after a full season of systematic, consistent recording. By that point, you have a personalised database of your competitive experience that contains more genuine insight into your own game than any external coaching assessment could provide.

You will know, from your documented evidence, which self-regulation strategies have worked most consistently for you under pressure. You will know the specific tactical patterns that have been most effective against specific types of opponents. You will know the court conditions in which your serve is most and least reliable. You will know the emotional patterns that precede your best and worst performances. You will know, in writing, what your cue words are and whether they are working.

This knowledge is not generic. It is specific to you, built from your experience, and applicable to your future performance in a way that no book - including this one - can replicate. The journal is where this book's strategies meet your individual competitive reality. Use it.

CHAPTER 37

When It All Falls Apart Anyway

> 💡 **PRACTICAL TIP:** Life happens, be kind to yourself.

What to do when every tool in this book fails you

You have read thirty-six chapters. You have learned to breathe in fours, to walk slowly, to press your toes into your shoes, to find the centre of the net cord with your eyes, to shake out your arms and reset your grip and nod quietly to yourself between points. You have, in some sense, done everything right.

And then the match begins ... and none of it works.

The breath comes shallow and fast regardless. The shoulders won't drop. The grip tightens no matter how many times you consciously release it. The emotional spike arrives like a wave and nothing, not the towel ritual, not the back fence, not the deliberate bounce of the ball, seems to reach it in time. You miss a shot you have hit ten thousand times in training. Then another. The lead evaporates. The head fills with noise. And somewhere in the middle of it all, you are not the composed, self-regulating player this book described. You are just a person, overwhelmed, on a court, losing.

This chapter is for that moment.

The Nervous System Does Not Always Cooperate

Here is a truth that sports psychology sometimes skirts around carefully but that every competitive player already knows in their body: self-regulation is a skill, and like all skills, it can fail under sufficient pressure. The tools in this book are real, and they work, but they are not guarantees. They are probabilities. They shift the odds in your favour. They give you more good matches than you would otherwise have, more composure than you would otherwise feel, more clarity than the moment deserves. But the nervous system is not a machine that responds to correct inputs with correct outputs every time. It is a living, fluctuating, context-sensitive system, shaped by sleep and stress and the score and the surface and the opponent and a thousand other variables operating below conscious awareness.

Sometimes, the body simply does not respond the way you trained it to. This is not a failure of the tools. It is not a failure of you. It is the nature of high-stakes human performance.

The greatest players who have ever lived have stood on that exact same ground.

The Greats Who Lost the Plot

On 22 June 1981, on the most famous tennis court in the world, John McEnroe stood on Centre Court at Wimbledon during his first-round match against fellow American Tom Gullikson and uttered words that would echo through sporting history for the next four decades.

McEnroe had served what he believed to be an ace. The ball landed on the line and chalk sprayed visibly into the air, yet chair umpire Edward James called it out. McEnroe approached the net, fury rising. *"You can't be serious, man. YOU CANNOT BE SERIOUS!"* he raged. *"That ball is on the line. Chalk flew up. It was clearly in. How can you possibly call that out?"*

The tirade escalated. Later in the same match, McEnroe directed his anger at the chair umpire again, calling James *"the absolute pits of the world."* He was docked a point, fined, and threatened with disqualification. Replays suggested he may well have been right about the call.

Despite the controversy, he went on to win the tournament, defeating Bjorn Borg in the final to claim the first of his three Wimbledon titles. The phrase became so iconic that McEnroe later used it as the title of his 2002 autobiography.

It is one of the most instructive moments in the history of the sport, not because it showed that losing emotional control is acceptable, but because it revealed something important: even catastrophic emotional dysregulation does not necessarily end the story. McEnroe's nervous system had overwhelmed his composure entirely. His behaviour was, in his own later admission, embarrassing. And yet the competitor in him survived it, regrouped, and won a Grand Slam. The meltdown was not the final word. It never has to be.

Daniil Medvedev's third-round match against Feliciano López at the 2019 US Open on 30 August, played at Louis Armstrong Stadium in New York, descended into chaos when Medvedev snatched a towel from a ball person and was issued a code violation by chair umpire Damien Dumusois. He then threw his racquet in the direction of the umpire's chair and, as he walked past it, made an obscene gesture toward the umpire, caught on camera and broadcast on the stadium screen. The New York crowd, already hostile, erupted in boos.

Medvedev was fined $9,000 for those offences across the match. And yet he won, and then turned to face the crowd in his post-match speech with a line that has never been forgotten: *"I want all of you to know when you sleep tonight, I won because of you. All the energy you're giving me right now, the more you do this, the more I will win for you guys."*

He acknowledged afterwards that the situation had got the better of him: *"I was in the heat of the moment. Started losing the momentum, and it was tough."* He went on to reach the final of that same US Open, losing to Rafael Nadal in five extraordinary sets.

Nick Kyrgios has provided some of the most documented emotional meltdowns in modern tennis. At the 2019 Cincinnati Masters, during a heated match against Karen Khachanov, Kyrgios took a bathroom break and smashed two racquets in the corridor, out of public view, but not out of earshot. He called the chair umpire a "tool" during the match. The total financial fallout from his conduct that tournament reached $113,000 in fines.

At the 2022 Miami Open against Jannik Sinner, in the fourth round, Kyrgios grew increasingly frustrated with umpire Carlos Bernardes. After receiving a point penalty for telling a friend in the crowd that he could do a better job at officiating (point penalty for verbal conduct) Kyrgios continued arguing. He lost the first set in a tiebreak and received a game penalty for continued verbal abuse. He then smashed his racquet several times and was subsequently fined $35,000 for his behaviour.

Later that same year, at the 2022 US Open against Karen Khachanov, following a quarter-final defeat, Kyrgios lost his temper and smashed two racquets in quick succession on the court itself, a raw, public act of frustration that was broadcast to millions. This resulted in him being fined an additional $14,000 for the destruction of the racquets.

And yet, in that same year of 2022, Kyrgios reached the Wimbledon final as an unseeded player, navigating the entire draw without the protection of a seeding, defeating high-ranked opponents along the way, including a deeply contentious third-round win against Stefanos Tsitsipas that drew widespread criticism for his behaviour. In his first-round match alone he was fined over $14,000, including a penalty for spitting in the direction of a spectator. The chaos and the brilliance arrived together, as they always had. He lost the final to Novak Djokovic 4–6, 6–3, 6–4, 7–6(3), but the run itself was remarkable by any measure. In the years prior, Kyrgios had spoken openly about serious mental health struggles, including self-harm and suicidal thoughts, context that makes his 2022 fortnight at Wimbledon something more than a tennis story.

He had been known, in quieter moments, to hand broken racquets to young fans in the crowd after his outbursts, a strange, disarming tenderness sitting alongside the fury. He carried all of it, every fine, every headline, every breakdown, onto the most famous courts in the world, and still produced the tennis of his life. His career offers one clear and factual lesson for every junior player who has ever lost control on a court: a history of losing composure does not disqualify you from greatness. It happened. He kept playing. That is the whole point.

Perhaps the most visually extraordinary equipment meltdown in tennis history, however, belongs not to a player in the heat of a contested rally, but to Marcos Baghdatis, sitting calmly in his chair at a changeover.

At the 2012 Australian Open on Margaret Court Arena, Baghdatis found himself two sets down and a break behind in the third against Stanislas Wawrinka. What happened next has never quite been matched for sheer spectacle. Baghdatis picked up his racquet and smashed it into the court surface. Then again. Then again, seven times in total. He then reached into his bag, removed a brand-new, still-wrapped racquet, and smashed that one too. Then another. Then a fourth. Four racquets destroyed in under a minute, the last three of them never having struck a single ball in their lives. The footage went viral almost immediately and remains one of the most-watched moments in tennis history. What made it stranger still was what followed: Baghdatis composed himself, walked back onto the court, and won the third set 7–5. The outburst, whatever it cost him internally, appeared to release something. He lost the match regardless, eventually going down 7–6(3), 6–4, 5–7, 6–1, and was fined for equipment abuse, a figure that seemed almost comically modest given the scale of the destruction.

There was speculation in the days that followed that the outburst carried additional weight beyond the match itself: Baghdatis had reportedly been dropped by his racquet sponsor Tecnifibre just weeks earlier, lending the systematic demolition of four of their products a certain unspoken dimension. Whether or not that was a factor, what the Baghdatis moment illustrates, alongside McEnroe, Medvedev, and Kyrgios, is that the emotional pressure of professional tennis does not spare the experienced, the gifted, or the composed. It finds everyone eventually. The question is never whether you will have a moment. The question is what you do with it afterwards.

What Actually Happens in the Body

When the self-regulation tools stop working, it is almost always because the physiological arousal has exceeded what the techniques, in that moment, can reach. Box breathing works best when initiated early, before the spike becomes a flood. The between-point routine works best when it has been repeated so many thousands of times that it runs almost automatically. The grounding techniques work best when there is still a thread of composure to anchor them to.

But when the cortisol and adrenaline load becomes high enough, when the accumulated stress of the match, the score, the crowd, the expectation, the tiredness, and the history between you and a particular opponent all converge at once, the brain's prefrontal cortex, the seat of rational decision-making and deliberate self-control, effectively goes offline. Temporarily. Not permanently. But enough that the tools feel unreachable, like knowing there is a fire extinguisher on the wall but being unable to find the wall.

This is not weakness. It is neuroscience. It happens to professionals who have spent their entire careers training for exactly these moments. It will sometimes happen to you.

The question is never whether the breakdown happens. The question is what you do with it afterwards, in the moment, across the match, and in the long arc of your development as a player.

In the Moment: The Only Things That Still Work

When everything else fails, a few simple anchors tend to remain accessible even deep in a stress response. They are not elegant. They are not sophisticated. But they are real.

Take one breath. Not four. Not a box. Just one deliberate breath. Inhale. Exhale. That is all.

Move your feet. Take three or four steps in any direction. Movement, even aimless movement, interrupts the frozen, locked quality of a full emotional spiral.

Say nothing. The most damaging thing a player in a dysregulated state can do is speak, to the umpire, to the opponent, to themselves aloud. The words that come out in those moments are almost never the words you would choose. Close the mouth. Keep moving. Wait.

And perhaps most importantly: *let the point go.* Not the match. Not your dignity. Not your commitment to the next point. Just that one point. It has happened. It cannot be revised. The only currency left is the next one.

After the Match: The Hardest and Most Important Conversation

When a match has gone wrong, when the emotional wheels came off and the tools failed and you behaved in ways you would not choose to repeat, there is a conversation that needs to happen. Not with your coach first. Not with your parents. With yourself.

Not a punishing conversation. Not a spiral of self-criticism that rehearses every mistake in forensic detail. A quiet, honest one.

What triggered it? At what point did I lose the thread? Was there a moment where one of the tools might have caught it, if I had reached for it sooner? What will I do differently in the next tight moment?

This is not analysis for its own sake. It is the process by which a player who lost control today builds the habit that holds them together next month. The Tennis Match Journal in the previous chapter exists precisely for this purpose. Use it after the hard matches, not just the good ones. The difficult entries are the ones that teach you the most.

A Final Word

This book has given you tools. Real tools, grounded in physiology and psychology and the hard-earned experience of players and coaches who have stood where you are standing. But tools are not the same as certainty, and certainty was never the promise.

The promise was this: that if you build these habits consistently, practice them until they are woven into your game, and return to them patiently after every match, whether it went well or went sideways, you will become, over time, a player who handles pressure better than you did before. Not perfectly. Not without setbacks. But better. Meaningfully, measurably better.

John McEnroe had some of the most spectacular meltdowns in the history of professional tennis. He also won seven Grand Slam singles titles, was ranked world number one for a combined 170 weeks and is widely regarded as one of the most gifted players the sport has ever produced. His composure was not the source of his greatness. His relentlessness was. The refusal to let a bad moment become the final moment.

You are allowed to fall apart sometimes. You are allowed to miss the breath cue, skip the back fence, squeeze the grip too tight, and say something to yourself between points that this book would not recommend. You are allowed to be human in the middle of a match that feels like it means everything.

What you are asked to do, the only thing this book ultimately asks, is to come back. To the tools, to the habits, to the practice, to the next match, to the version of yourself that is still growing.

Progress is not perfection. It never was. A player who loses control and reflects on it afterwards is further along than a player who never examined their game at all. A player who tries the box breathing and feels nothing on Tuesday might feel it catch on Thursday. The nervous system learns slowly, and it learns through repetition, not through single perfect performances.

The lessons in this book extend well beyond a junior tennis court. Consider Lewis Hamilton at the 2021 Abu Dhabi Grand Prix. Hamilton had led for 1,296 of the race's 1,297 laps, a statistic that remains one of the most striking in motorsport history. He was on the cusp of a record-breaking eighth World Championship. Then, in the final lap, a late safety car and a controversial restart handed Max Verstappen the position and, with it, the title. Hamilton became the only driver ever to win and lose a World Championship on the final lap of a season. By almost any measure, it was one of the most painful sporting losses imaginable, not because he had performed poorly, but because he had performed brilliantly. The outcome simply did not reflect it.

What followed said everything about the champion he is. Rather than disappearing into bitterness or public grievance, Hamilton returned carrying the words *Still I Rise*, a phrase so central to his identity that he has had it embroidered on the back of his helmets and tattooed on his shoulders, drawn from the Maya Angelou poem of the same name. He did not pretend the loss had not happened. He did not minimise how devastating it was. He acknowledged it, processed it, and came back. That is not a story about winning. It is a story about what kind of person you choose to be after the hardest moments, and it is exactly the kind of mindset that separates those who keep growing from those who stop.

For a junior tennis player, a parent on the fence, or a coach on the sideline: the scoreline will not always be fair. The calls will not always go your way. There will be matches, and perhaps seasons, where the result does not reflect the effort or the quality of the person playing. What matters, in those moments, is the choice you make about what comes next. *Still I Rise* is not just a phrase. It is a posture toward competition and toward life. And it is available to every player who has ever walked off a court feeling like the outcome was not the whole story… because it never is.

Keep going. Keep practising. Keep coming back.

The next match is waiting.

REFERENCES & FURTHER READING

The strategies and principles in this book draw on a broad base of research in sports psychology, neuroscience, motor learning, and clinical psychology. The following texts and areas of research are recommended for readers who wish to explore the theoretical foundations of competitive self-regulation in greater depth.

Sports Psychology & Performance

Kahneman, D. (2011). *Thinking, Fast and Slow*. Farrar, Straus and Giroux.

Gallwey, W.T. (1974). *The Inner Game of Tennis*. Random House.

Csikszentmihalyi, M. (1990). *Flow: The Psychology of Optimal Experience*. Harper & Row.

Duckworth, A. (2016). *Grit: The Power of Passion and Perseverance*. Scribner.

Byrne, R. (2006). *The Secret*. Atria Books.

Neuroscience & Embodied Cognition

van der Kolk, B. (2014). *The Body Keeps the Score*. Viking.

Porges, S.W. (2011). *The Polyvagal Theory*. Norton.

Carney, D.R., Cuddy, A.J.C., & Yap, A.J. (2010). *Power Posing: Brief Nonverbal Displays Affect Neuroendocrine Levels and Risk Tolerance*. Psychological Science.

Motor Learning & Skill Acquisition

Ericsson, K.A. (2016). *Peak: Secrets from the New Science of Expertise*. Houghton Mifflin Harcourt.

Masters, R.S.W. (1992). *Knowledge, knerves and know-how: The role of explicit versus implicit knowledge in the breakdown of a complex motor skill under pressure*. British Journal of Psychology.

Duhigg, C. (2012). *The Power of Habit: Why We Do What We Do in Life and Business*. Random House.

Breathing & Autonomic Regulation

Zaccaro, A., et al. (2018). *How Breath-Control Can Change Your Life: A Systematic Review on Psycho-Physiological Correlates of Slow Breathing*. Frontiers in Human Neuroscience.

Jerath, R., et al. (2006). *Physiology of Long Pranayamic Breathing*. Medical Hypotheses.

Mindfulness in Sport

Gardner, F.L. & Moore, Z.E. (2007). *The Psychology of Enhancing Human Performance: The Mindfulness-Acceptance-Commitment (MAC) Approach*. Springer.

Williams, M. & Penman, D. (2011). *Mindfulness: A Practical Guide to Finding Peace in a Frantic World*. Piatkus.